ONTARIO WORKS —
WORKS FOR WHOM?

ONTARIO WORKS — WORKS FOR WHOM?

An Investigation of Workfare in Ontario

JULIE VAILLANCOURT

Fernwood Publishing • Halifax and Winnipeg

Copyright © 2010 Julie Vaillancourt

Editing and design: Brenda Conroy
Cover design: John van der Woude
Printed and bound in Canada by Hignell Book Printing

 Mixed Sources
Product group from well-managed
forests and other controlled sources
www.fsc.org Cert no. SW-COC-003438
© 1996 Forest Stewardship Council

Published in Canada by Fernwood Publishing
32 Oceanvista Lane
Black Point, Nova Scotia, B0J 1B0
and #8 – 222 Osborne Street, Winnipeg, Manitoba, R3L 1Z3
www.fernwoodpublishing.ca

Fernwood Publishing Company Limited gratefully acknowledges the financial support of the Government of Canada through the Canada Book Fund, the Canada Council for the Arts and the Nova Scotia Department of Tourism and Culture for our publishing program.

 Canadian Patrimoine
Heritage canadien
  The Canada Council for the Arts
Le Conseil des Arts du Canada
 NOVA SCOTIA
Tourism and Culture

Library and Archives Canada Cataloguing in Publication

Vaillancourt, Julie, 1982-
Ontario works – works for whom?: an investigation of Workfare in Ontario /
Julie Vaillancourt.

Includes bibliographical references.
ISBN 978-1-55266-351-6

1. Welfare recipients—Employment—Ontario. 2. Public welfare administration--
Ontario. I. Title.

HV109.O54V35 2010   362.5'8409713   C2010-900012-9

CONTENTS

Acknowledgments 7

Introduction 9
    Note.. 13

1 Welfare within the Capitalist System 15
    Capitalism 15
    Relief Arrangements...................................... 16
    Neoliberalism 17
    The Common Sense Revolution..................... 18
    Summary.. 20
    Note.. 21

2 Problems in the Everyday Lives of Recipients..................... 23
    Social Assistance Recipients.............................. 23
    Social Relations that Push People onto Assistance.............. 28
    Problems Specific to Raising Children on Assistance.......... 33
    Summary.. 36
    Note.. 37

3 Enforcing Work Norms 39
    Administrative Obstacles 39
    Lessons for Others.. 48
    Pressure to Work for Low Wages 53
    Summary.. 56
    Notes 57

4 Ontario Works — Program Priorities 59

    Ontario Works Purpose 59

    Becoming and Staying Employed 61

    Defining Employability 63

    Individualizing Poverty 66

    Work of the Brokers 67

    Placement Programs 68

    Summary 74

    Notes 75

5 Problems for Participating Organizations 77

    Struggles against Workfare 77

    The Decision to Participate 80

    Experiences on Placement 86

    Summary 93

    Notes 93

6 Meeting the Needs of Social Assistance Recipients 95

    The Social Organization of Ontario Works 95

    Contributions and Implications of this Study 98

    Social Assistance and Workfare Programs 102

    Further Research Is Necessary 103

    Recommendations for Change 104

    Notes 107

References 109

ACKNOWLEDGMENTS

This project would not have been possible without the assistance from the people who shared their stories with me. For your kindness, your openness and your insights, I thank you. I also wish to thank Drs. Gary Kinsman, Mercedes Steedman and Kate Tilleczek for their guidance. Thanks are also due to my family and my friends (with special thanks to my husband Roch) for putting up with me as I worked through this.

INTRODUCTION

This book is about the Ontario Works program and the problems it creates in the lives of people on social assistance. Ontario Works is the work-for-welfare (workfare) program that was implemented in Ontario in 1996 as part of the neoliberal restructuring of the welfare state. Workfare is a broad term used to refer to many different programs, the basic characteristic of which is that recipients of social assistance are required to work for their benefits, either through employment, community placements or educational initiatives (Quaid 2002: 3). Workfare programs are usually implemented under the guise of helping people "transition" from social assistance into paid employment, and they are almost always mandatory and coercive.[1]

There are a number of complaints and problems that arise within discussions about the Ontario Works program. This book focuses on the work-for-welfare requirement and the "employment assistance services" that were implemented as part of the program. My analysis shows that the actual objective of Ontario Works has nothing to do with helping people on social assistance or providing people with "real jobs," as is claimed in official discourse. Rather, the program has to do with facilitating an attack on people on social assistance more generally, while providing subsidized labour for some companies and social agencies. This labour is provided in precarious and transient forms that are not going to produce any major benefits in the lives of people on social assistance.

My interest in the Ontario Works program stems from my personal experience with a similar program. After completing my bachelor's degree and relocating to a new city to follow my partner, I started receiving Employment Insurance. During this time, I voluntarily signed-up for a program where I worked thirty-five hours a week for a local organization and my EI benefits became in effect my paycheque. Despite having volunteered for the program, I could not leave without losing my "eligibility" for benefits, even though I found the experience not very useful as I spent much of my time doing tedious work, such as stuffing envelopes and photocopying. Furthermore, the hours I spent in this program impeded my ability to search for a "real" job.

This book is based on my master's thesis, which was an institutional ethnography of the Ontario Works program. The foundation of this book rests upon the experiences of six social assistance recipients, who shared with me their experiences with the program. My aim was to take up their critical standpoint in relation to the Ontario Works program and the problems it creates in their everyday lives. I also spoke with people who work in administering part of the program (brokers) and with people from participating organizations (organizations that "host" Ontario Works placements).

In total, I interviewed seventeen research participants for this project: six social assistance recipients, three brokers and eight people from participating organizations. I conducted semi-structured in-person interviews with all participants using three separate interview guides — one for each group of respondents. I chose a semi-structured interview format to enable the flexibility to explore topics as they arose (Smith 2006: 23).

I started by interviewing two Ontario Works recipients in order to construct a standpoint of how the program worked from their perspective. My third and fourth interviews were with people from participating organizations, and the next three interviews were with brokers. This staggering of interviews allowed me to start with an understanding of the program from the point of view of recipients and to begin to see how problems were organized in their lives. Starting with their experiences allowed me to identify institutional relations that are important in coordinating people's experience and to further explore these in subsequent interviews with participants from different social locations. The remaining interviews were a mix of recipients and people from participating organizations.

This book also uses quantitative information from secondary sources to complement some of my arguments. It is important to note that the statistics included are only as good as the methods used to collect them. Also, some of the figures are provided from institutional standpoints and so their language and definitions can be problematic.

I recruited people to participate in this study through personal contacts, who then forwarded the invitation to other people from the groups I was targeting. I encountered some difficulties in recruiting Ontario Works recipients and the method that yielded the best response was having people referred to me through their friends and acquaintances. Once my contacts were made, they were certainly very open in teaching me about the Ontario Works program. All but one of them invited me into their homes, and nobody hesitated to answer any of my questions about how the program works.

I was interested in speaking both with people from organizations that had accepted placements from Ontario Works and people from organizations that, for whatever reason, chose not to. This group was certainly the easiest to recruit because of my own social location; working for a social service agency, I had numerous contacts with other organizations.

The group that was hardest to recruit were people who worked in administering the program. I tried to speak with people from this group to gain an understanding of how the program operates from their work perspective. I only managed to speak with people who worked as brokers (and thus only administer part of the program) because senior administration would not allow Ontario Works case workers to participate in my project (and senior administration did not return any of my follow-up phone calls). Inside sources tell me that the reluctance came from the fact that the Ontario Works program is a provincial program and that the program itself is very prescriptive. In other words, I would learn all I need to know about how the program operates from reading the program directives (guiding program documents). In speaking with the research participants, I learned that although the program is prescriptive, there are opportunities for discretionary decision-making in how the program is applied. It is therefore unfortunate that I was not able to speak to Ontario Works case workers directly. Because of this, I was not able to learn about the practical work-based knowledge they use in their work and how they activate or bring to life the program directives (Smith 2006: 82). All three brokers interviewed were from the same broker agency and the interviews were conducted at the broker agency itself.

The book explores what these interviews and other information have shown me about how the Ontario Works program is socially organized from the standpoint of social assistance recipients. In chapter one, I briefly situate welfare within the capitalist system and give an overview of the origins and development of the Ontario Works program. In chapter two I begin critically analyzing the Ontario Works program from the standpoint of the social assistance recipients with whom I spoke, exploring some of the social relations that pushed them onto social assistance and some of the problems they face specific to raising children on assistance. I also provide some insight into the problems they experience in their everyday lives as a result of the Ontario Works program.

Chapter three explores how the Ontario Works program comes to serve the needs of the ruling relations of capital at the expense of people living in poverty. This is achieved by examining how the Ontario Works program serves to enforce work norms by a series of administrative obstacles that make it difficult for people to obtain or stay on social assistance, by using social assistance recipients to provide a lesson to people who work for wages that their fate on social assistance would be worse than in any low paying job and by pressuring social assistance recipients to work for low wages.

In chapter four, I discuss some of the conceptual practices behind the Ontario Works program as they are revealed through key texts from the program. This is achieved largely through an examination of the priorities that emerge from a critical textual analysis of the program and from speaking with people who work in administering the program. This chapter highlights that the actual intent of the program has nothing to do with helping social assistance recipients. Here I explore how Ontario Works is part of a broader neoliberal attack on people living in poverty that is based on disciplining the poor and regulating their morals.

Chapter five builds on the knowledge of people working for participating organizations and discusses what they revealed about how the program is socially organized. The participants have shown me how state regulations attempt to involve these organizations in the moral regulation of people on social assistance and they highlighted a number of problems with practices in the Ontario Works program. This chapter also explores some of the early struggles against workfare.

In the final chapter, I summarize the main findings from the research and examine the main contributions it makes. This includes a social map of the Ontario Works program and a review of the main social relations that serve to organize the program, and to which the program contributes. I also highlight the implications of this study as they relate to the lives of social assistance recipients and social assistance and workfare programs. Finally, I provide recommendations for change.

NOTE

1.   Quaid (2002: 23) argues that there has been a widening of what programs fall under the term "workfare" and that the "new-style" workfare "now refers to a wide range of strategies that help able-bodied welfare recipients make the transition from reliance on welfare to economic independence" (these include both mandatory and voluntary programs).

Chapter 1

WELFARE WITHIN
THE CAPITALIST SYSTEM

This chapter briefly reviews some key points related to the system of capitalism and looks at how welfare is situated within this system. This is followed by an overview of neoliberalism and how this has affected welfare within the capitalist system. The last part of this chapter looks at key excerpts from the "Common Sense Revolution" that highlight the extent to which the welfare reforms that led to the Ontario Works program were part of the neoliberal agenda, which aims to undermine social security programs and force people to work cheaply.

CAPITALISM

Capitalism is a social relation based on the exploitation of surplus value from workers. According to Marx, the history of current society is based on class struggle. Put simply, the main opposing classes are the bourgeoisie (the dominant class) and the proletariat (the working class, which includes people living in poverty). Conflict arises because these groups have competing interests; capitalists wish to maximize their profits based on the exploitation of human labour power, while workers wish to minimize or abolish this exploitation. It is important to see that value is exploited both from waged and unwaged labour. Domestic and reproductive work within the home, such as performing housework and raising children, also contributes to the social relations of capital and to the creation of surplus value as they produce the labour power of the working class, which is the active force in capitalist relations of production (Kinsman 2005: 41).

Cycles of capitalist accumulation consistently generate poverty and unemployment. Capitalist social relations do not create enough employment for everyone, and the appropriation of surplus value from workers results in a section of the working class (both waged and unwaged) who are living in poverty. This group of workers, along with the unemployed population, are considered necessary in a capitalist society. Not only is surplus value extracted from their unpaid labour, which produces and reproduces labour power for capitalist relations, but they also form what Marx called the "industrial reserve army of labour." Essentially these people represent the labourers who are available for the new jobs that are created — most of which, in recent times, are in the services sector.

RELIEF ARRANGEMENTS

Under capitalism, it is claimed that the state's role is to mediate conflict between classes by protecting the rights of workers. However, this is not the case in reality, as state relations generally operate in the interest of capital. This is evidenced by the fact that (similar to the argument put forth about the health sector by Renaud 1975: 559) capitalism creates problems such as poverty and unemployment, which are subject to state regulation, which "make[s] the solutions to these needs [problems] compatible with the capitalist organization of the economy." Relief arrangements clearly exemplify this. As is explored throughout this book, the Ontario Works program exemplifies a government policy purported to help people living in poverty, which in fact is favourable to capitalists at the expense of the poor. This example highlights the extent to which "[the state] is not an arbiter between social classes, but an element in the class system itself" (Renaud 1975: 565).

Piven and Cloward argue that relief arrangements are enacted as a means to regulate the people in the reserve army of labour. The logic here is that certain institutions are able to exert control over individuals who need aid to survive because their failure to act in certain ways will result in the loss of assistance (Piven and Cloward 1993: 22). According to Piven and Cloward, there are two types of relief arrangements, expansive and restrictive, and each serves a different purpose for broader economic and social relations. They argue that "relief policies are cyclical ... depending on the problems of regulation in the larger society with which government must contend" and that "expansive relief policies are designed to mute civil disorder, and restrictive ones to reinforce work norms" (1993: xv). Expansive relief policies are won by the working class, and they are enacted to appease the people who are left unemployed due to constantly changing needs of the waged labour market. Relief is given by the state in hopes that it will "forestall disorder" and prevent the poor from rebelling until wage labour needs rise again. Restrictive relief policies are of interest for this research because this category is where we find workfare policies such as Ontario Works, which serve to reinforce work norms.

NEOLIBERALISM

Capitalism has gone through different phases and each phase has greatly influenced corresponding relief arrangements. Neoliberalism is the capitalist phase during which workfare policies such as Ontario Works were introduced. Neoliberalism is a particularly aggressive application of capitalism that is favourable to business at the expense of workers. Under neoliberalism social security programs are attacked and measures are implemented to create a more disciplined workforce.

Neoliberal policies represent a marked departure from the economic and social theory of Keynesianism, which influenced policy-making after the Second World War. The social reforms that emerged during this time were congruent with the notions expressed by the British economist John Maynard Keynes and focused on relations within the national economy. These policies were aimed at reducing unemployment and increasing consumption through state intervention (Smith and Smith 1990: 174–75). Essentially, Keynesian reforms were expansive relief arrangements in that they provided limited social benefits to working class and poor people in order to keep up a certain level of demand (thus also maintaining order by preventing rebellion from the poor).

In 1970s policies began to shift towards neoliberalism as a result of the "internationalization of capital" and the "coming of the global economy." Without a national home for capital, the notion of national economy was lost, and state regulations shifted away from maintaining employment and consumption towards ensuring that capital is able to compete on a global scale. At the national level this means being able to attract capital investment, in light of global competition; this is achieved by implementing policies that favour the social relations of capital and in some cases removing or reducing policies such as welfare that are not so favourable. Under neoliberalism the "social wage" is seen as giving too much power to workers and the poor; there is a need to attack workers and union rights as well as the "social wage" (including social assistance), to force workers to accept lower paid positions and to create conditions for increasing exploitation and enforcing work norms. As I examine shortly, these are some of the goals behind the Ontario Works program.

THE COMMON SENSE REVOLUTION

In the run up to the 1995 Ontario general election, the Progressive Conservative Party, led by Mike Harris, released its Common Sense Revolution election platform, which contained the welfare reforms that led to the Ontario Works program. The premise of this platform lay in the assumptions that "government isn't working anymore" and that "the system is broken." What Harris's party purported to offer was "a Common Sense Revolution in the way our province is run" (Harris 1995: 1). This "revolution" rested on five key components, the second of which — cutting government spending — is where welfare reform fits in.

Neoliberalism was openly alive and well in this election platform. This chapter presents a few key excerpts from the Common Sense Revolution document that exemplify this (and believe me there are many more). These excerpts demonstrate the extent to which state relations aimed to create policies that favoured the interest of the capitalists at the expense of people living in poverty.

The following quote outlines the purported goal of the welfare reforms, as presented in the Common Sense Revolution:

> We want to open up new opportunities and restore hope for people by breaking the cycle of dependency. That will be the goal of our welfare reform. The best social assistance program ever created is a real job, and this plan will generate hundreds of thousands of those. In the meantime, we must move to control costs and help people return to the workforce. (Harris 1995: 9)

Despite claiming that the goals will be to "restore hope" and "break the cycle of dependency," the main focus in the reforms is on pushing people off social assistance and into waged work (which does not necessarily achieve either goal). This is consistent with neoliberalism as it places increased pressure on people receiving social assistance to work for low wages. This benefits employers looking for cheap workers but does not necessarily address any of the social relations that push people onto social assistance.

The plan makes it clear that under these proposed reforms working will be mandatory:

> We should prepare welfare recipients to return to the workforce by requiring all able-bodied recipients — with the exception of single parents with young children — either to work, or to be retrained in return for their benefits. (Harris 1995: 9)

Clearly, working is being presented as the only option. This approach overlooks the work that people are already doing (such as child care and volunteer work), but it also disregards the fact that a number of people on social assistance are unable to work for wages. For instance, in 2003, 67 percent of the 29,000 applicants for the Ontario Disability Support Program (ODSP)[1] were Ontario Works recipients (Ministry of Community and Social Services 2004: 92). And although the above excerpt states that single parents with young children would be excluded, program statistics presented in chapter three show that in practice this is not the case.

Requiring participants to work is the supposed solution that will help to "fix" people receiving social assistance so that they are able to become "productive." The main problem is that despite trying to "fix" people receiving social assistance by mandating them to perform work, this solution does nothing to get at the social roots of poverty. In fact, the solution itself, and the entire Common Sense Revolution, completely overlook the social conditions that have resulted in people living in poverty. Rather, they obscure oppression and inequality and hide the class conflict at the core of this struggle. This serves to turn the collective issue of poverty into an individual problem, thus mandating solutions at the individual level.

The introduction to the plan claims that it is based on public consultations.

> Over the last few years I have been out talking with the people
> of Ontario. In Town Hall meetings, in living rooms and around
> kitchen tables. I have heard your message. (Harris 1995: 1)

One needs to question whose interests are being considered in this plan,
which is presented as though it responds to the needs of the "less for-
tunate and disadvantaged" (whom most would assume includes social
assistance recipients): The following excerpt makes clearer the middle-
class standpoint the Common Sense Revolution actually takes up. It is
not the standpoint of people living in poverty or of the working-class
generally.

> The policies in this plan have been in development for almost
> four years. They are designed to meet the ongoing concerns
> of Ontarians about the future of our economy. They respond
> to the needs of the middle class for job creation, tax relief and
> more efficient government, and the needs of the less fortunate
> and disadvantaged for more hope, opportunity and long-term
> security. (Harris 1995: 4)

According to the Common Sense Revolution, the idea for workfare
comes from the people of Ontario, further bringing into question who
was included in the consultations:

> You have told us that you want to replace welfare with a work,
> education and training social policy that rewards individual
> initiative and demands responsible behaviour from recipients
> of public assistance, even as it expands opportunities to achieve
> self-sufficiency. (Harris 1995: 9)

It is unlikely that the "you" being referenced here are people on social
assistance. As my interviews with social assistance recipients show, the
social relations that pushed them into poverty and onto social assistance
are not addressed in this plan.

SUMMARY

Capitalism and more specifically the neoliberal application of capitalism
are important lenses through which to explore welfare programs. These
concepts help to guide the investigation towards certain social relations

that need to be examined. A critical analysis of capitalism is helpful for its emphasis on the exploitation of the working class within the social relations of capital. An understanding of neoliberalism is important because it orients attention to some of the changes that attempt to morally regulate workers by attacking and dismantling social programs, thereby ensuring that workers are forced to work cheaply. Neoliberal elements are clearly present in the Common Sense Revolution, which furthers the interests of the dominant class at the expense of people living in poverty.

NOTE

1. This is the social assistance program in Ontario that provdes financial assistance to people with disabilities.

Chapter 2

PROBLEMS IN THE EVERYDAY LIVES OF RECIPIENTS

This chapter briefly introduces each of the social assistance recipients with whom I spoke. I then explore some of the social relations that push people onto social assistance, from the standpoint of social assistance recipients. These include lack of full-time employment, lack of access to higher education, lack of jobs that provide health benefits and discrimination. I also highlight some of the problems that recipients face that are specific to raising children on assistance, as all the recipients who participated in my research were parents. These include the difficulties their children face in escaping poverty as they reach adulthood, the pain of watching children be disappointed because their parents cannot afford things and the exclusion children face because of their parents' social locations.

SOCIAL ASSISTANCE RECIPIENTS

From the standpoint of state relations, the Ontario Works program is intended to "help people determine what they need to become employed" and "help people move as quickly as possible to a job and become self-reliant" (Ministry of Community and Social Services 2007). When I spoke with social assistance recipients, a disjuncture quickly emerged between how they related their experiences of the program and the official discourse from Ontario Works. Following is a brief introduction of the research participants who were Ontario Works recipients. I explore some of the disjunctures that emerged between their everyday experiences and the formal institutional ideologies of Ontario Works.

JILL

Jill is a social assistance recipient in her late forties. She is also a single mother of four children ranging in age from seventeen to twenty-five. Jill recently relocated to a medium sized city from a large urban centre. Jill has been on and off welfare all her adult life. She worked for wages when she could, and her perspective has always been: "That's the last thing that you should be on is the welfare system, you should have a job if there's one available."

She has no complaints about her experience with Ontario Works, and this is surprising given some of the work she has been required to do. But Jill has had a good case worker through Ontario Works and she says that makes a big difference. Unfortunately, Jill faced a number of obstacles in her life. Her marriage ended and she retained custody of the children. This experience pushes many women into poverty. She also had a "nervous breakdown." Additionally, a number of barriers have prevented her from getting a job, including lack of experience with certain kinds of work, lack of formal education and a learning disability.

> I have no experience with typing and stuff like that. Maybe I should go back to school. And that's another thing with Ontario Works; they encourage you to go to school. You know, if like myself you don't have an education. I have my grade nine, but I have like a dyslexia.

Despite having heard that Ontario Works encourages people to go to school, as part of her "employment assistance," Jill was never supported to go to school, not even to complete her high school diploma. And as opposed to giving her varied work experiences, her Ontario Works placement put her in a job where she was not learning new skills or gaining experience that would be helpful in getting her a job.

MELISSA AND JACK

Melissa and Jack are social assistance recipients living in a small town. They are a couple in their mid-thirties, with two school-aged children. They started receiving social assistance after the birth of their first child, about twelve years ago. Jack has been working on a part-time basis for the same employer for thirteen years. Unfortunately, he does not earn enough to support his family; nevertheless he continues to work there because he has not been able to find another job. Melissa left the waged workforce after the birth of her first child because the prospects that she faced were similar to Jack's, but also because she now had the work of raising a child. Jack is a high school graduate and Melissa has completed a college certificate program. The town in which they live presents limited employment opportunities, and they do not have a vehicle, which limits where they can search. Coupled with the fact that there is no public transportation in the area, this poses real constraints for them. Jack participated in three community placements, and Melissa completed two. They have decided to move to another province in hopes of a fresh start and a better life for their family.

Despite Ontario Works claiming to help people become employed, Melissa mentioned problems keeping employment because of the Ontario Works program.

> I've had a babysitting job on a very part-time basis, but I was still asked to do job searching. And that was basically after school hours so too many times I wasn't able to get out there and do what I had to do, but they were still telling me "You gotta do this there or you're not getting it [social assistance]" and there's only so much I can do.

Melissa had started providing child care services to others in her neighbourhood, both before and after school. Unfortunately, she had to stop this as it made it difficult for her to search for jobs and attend her community placement.

MARGARET
Margaret is forty-nine years old and she has been on social assistance for thirty years. She has raised two children on the system. Her daughter is now twenty-four and her son is thirty-two. She lives in a medium sized city. Once her youngest child was in school, she obtained her high school diploma. She then completed a college diploma while on assistance (something that is no longer possible under the Ontario Works system). Margaret has always had a part-time job since completing college, but it has never been enough for her to leave social assistance, and she has not been able to find a full-time job doing work she was trained for. In addition to her part-time job and her child rearing, Margaret volunteers for two local organizations. She is no longer on Ontario Works; she now receives financial support through the Ontario Disability Support Program (which provides a higher level of assistance).

Margaret also reported problems with keeping employment because of the Ontario Works program.

> I already had part-time contract work and I told them that the seventy hours [for the community placement] would interfere with my part-time work and they said that as long as I was on welfare I had to do it. So she [my worker] even suggested that I quit my part-time contract work that I was trained to do and look for a full-time job.

JANE

Jane is a forty-eight-year-old single mother of two, living in a medium sized city. Her son is twenty-six and he lives outside the home. He works in the restaurant industry, and he dropped out of school when he was sixteen. Jane's daughter is a sixteen-year-old high school student who lives at home with her mother. Jane has completed a grade twelve equivalency and she has been on and off assistance for the last twenty-five years — since her first pregnancy. She explains:

> Well I got pregnant in '82 and I was on unemployment and because I was showing in my fifth month, there was no way I could get a job. Nobody was gonna hire me when I was pregnant. So because maternity leave was right around the corner, I stayed on unemployment for a while 'til that ran out and then I had no choice but to go on welfare.

Jane has been required to participate in two community placements as part of the Ontario Works program. Jane has held a number of jobs, none of which have provided her with any job security, and correspondingly, none of them have lasted. She feels her age and her lack of formal education hold her back from getting a job.

Despite Ontario Works claiming to help recipients become self-sufficient, Jane describes how the program and its regulations reproduce relations of poverty intergenerationally. She explains that due to welfare regulations, her son was forced to move out at sixteen because he dropped out of high school.

> My son had dropped out of school when he was sixteen. They told me, my counsellor, my worker at welfare told me, that either he signs up for the [employment program], or he has to move out. He has to get a job, help out [with family expenses] or move out. Like who are they to tell you

your child has to move out? So my son had to move out, you know, which was sad because he's only sixteen. He wasn't ready to move out.

She worries about what will happen to her daughter in a few years once she graduates from high school. She will either be forced to move out as well or have to go on assistance herself. She would like her daughter to go to college or university, but it will be next to impossible because of how the welfare system currently works.

They [social assistance] only let the children live there [in the family home] as long as they're going to school, they'll cover them or until they turn eighteen. My daughter's going to be eighteen in two years, and she's going to school and that's the only reason she's still covered. Which is sad, very sad. What if she wants to go to college or university and live at home and go? The only way that she can stay is if she takes over half the rent. And like she's going to be going to school, how can she afford that?

LOUISE

Louise is in her early fifties. She is a mother of three, and she ended a bad marriage, which left her with the children. She has been on social assistance for a long time, and she has recently moved onto the Ontario Disability Support Program. She completed her high school diploma while on social assistance (before the change to Ontario Works). She suffers from mental illness and had been volunteering for a local organization that works with people who suffer from mental illness when workfare was announced. She became very nervous that she would be forced to work somewhere that she would not be able to "handle" because of her illness, so she volunteered to start a placement for the organization with which she was already volunteering. This led to a job, which she had to leave when her illness began preventing her from working. Louise describes her experience with the Ontario Works program as a modern-day form of slavery.

Well, I know it [the program]'s gone down to the toilet now. It's like $95, seventy hours [in community placements], you have to pay your own bus pass, it's ludicrous. It feels like slavery, just like slavery. Because you're a slave, you keep the person in a place and then you make sure they have the food, and just, just enough for little things and that's it. That's what it turned out to be, twentieth-century slavery or twenty-first, whatever it is.

Louise's children are now grown, and one of her daughters is now on assistance with three children of her own.

SOCIAL RELATIONS THAT PUSH PEOPLE ONTO ASSISTANCE

With a better understanding of where the social assistance recipients with whom I spoke are socially located, I now begin to explore some of the social relations that push people onto social assistance.

Workfare programs are supposedly used to give people the "push" that they need to work. This is based on the underlying assumption that people on social assistance are lazy. However, the people I met, like most people living in poverty, cannot be considered lazy. Every one of them worked, although not always in the formal capitalist system of production. All the people I spoke with were parents (which is true for almost half of all social assistance cases[1]). They are involved in the socially necessary work of raising children, but this is not acknowledged in the neoliberal perspective of what counts as work, despite the fact that these efforts play an important role in producing labour power as a commodity for exploitation within capitalist relations of production.

Contrary to the socially produced perception that social assistance recipients are lazy and do not want to work, all of the people I spoke with who were able to work for wages expressed a desire to do so. For example, Jack and Melissa have taken a drastic step in relocating their family in the hopes that they will be able to find work.

> Melissa: We tried and we're still not anywhere so therefore we're making the move to have something better. To have a fresh start. And if we can actually get something where we're both working full-time and be off assistance then all the better.

The reality for many people on social assistance is that they face barriers to employment and to obtaining a living wage. For example, for Jane, the barriers were insufficient formal education and a lack of jobs. She explains that during periods when she was providing care to terminally ill people she got paid less for doing the same job as others because she does not have a certificate or a diploma. She had to stop this type of work because it became difficult, mostly due to her age, but also emotionally.

My clientele kept dying off on me. I mean they're terminally ill, and then I have to go and find new clients. It wasn't too bad after a while because the [organization] and the hospital pretty much gave out my name and phone number.... but in the beginning it was almost impossible to get clients, because you have nurses, and retired nurses that do these jobs or nurses that take time off from the hospital to do these private jobs. You get paid more from these kinds of jobs. But because I didn't have any papers for it, I was only making $10 an hour, which was pretty good money back then. Now it's nothing. Back then it was pretty good. Sometimes I'd make $15 an hour. It all depended on the family. Like I said, my clients kept dying off and it was getting harder to deal with. You work with clients for six months, seven months before they die, so you get pretty close to them. And like the funerals I was going to was unbelievable, it was hard. It was like losing a real friend. Like I knew it was going to happen, but still kind of hard when it does. And like I did take it hard at times, and it was like one client would die, and I'd have to take a little bit of time off. Then look for a new client, and that takes time, because a lot of people would like professionals to help out with family members. It was just getting way too much, because you not only took care of the person but you took care of their duties at home. Like you'd do light housekeeping, the cooking, the laundry... It was pretty hard and I was getting older, so it was time to move on.

And it is not that she did not try. On the contrary, she had started a college course but had to drop out because of an accident. Not only did this leave her without a degree, but it also left her with a loan to repay.

You take out these loans [for school] and what happens if something happens to you and you can't finish the course. Just like I did, I took out a loan... and I had ended up in the hospital because I had an accident and I needed surgery, rehab and everything else. Where am I left? I missed six months because of rehab and being in the hospital, my course, so the course was over for me. I couldn't go back but here I had this loan out. So now you come out of rehab and you gotta get a job. And you're limited physically because you go from there and what do you end up with? Nada.

For others, like Jill, the lack of formal education can be complicated by other issues. In her case, she also had to contend with a learning disability and limited work experience, which restricted the kind of jobs she could apply for. Instead of assistance with completing high school or getting varied work experience or even receiving help for her learning disability, she was put in a placement where she worked to make parks and streets "safe" by picking up drug paraphernalia and discarded condoms. During the winter she also shovelled snow.

For people like Jack, Melissa, Jill and Margaret, the main problem has been a lack of available full-time employment. Melissa and Margaret, for example, had completed college degrees, yet were unable to find full-time work where they lived.

> Margaret: And then there's people like me, and other people that I know that have been educated that can't find a job in their field full-time for whatever reason, so there's gaps at both ends and we all don't just fit into this get on workfare, get a placement and score a job and right after you're off welfare. And they [the government] don't understand that.

Although it is true that Jill had not completed high school, she nevertheless was keen to get employment. Unfortunately, however, she had relocated to another city where job opportunities were scarce.

> It's like I said, you wanna work, it is hard to find work and I mean like I said, I come from [city name]. I've been in [new city name] for three years, going on three years this September. For me to find work, it is hard because they don't have the work here like they do in [previous city]. Especially my kind of work.

In addition to barriers tied to educational credentialism and employment availability, others faced discrimination tied to social values around appearance and age. Melissa reported barriers to employment because of her weight and her standard of clothing related to living in poverty. In the following excerpt, she describes an incident where she had little time to prepare for an interview, and she felt the employer had a problem with her footwear, which prevented her from getting the job.

> I've had quite a few interviews and every time in the last five years I've been refused to all of them. Why? Well apparently because, well for one of them my shoes weren't up to date... The day I went in with my résumé, well she calls me and says, "Can I see you at a certain time today?" Well

you don't really have time, when you're not expecting to receive a call, you can't really do anything. And by contacting the worker, there's not much they can do so... I went through the interview fine, she said "I'll call you in about three to four days." I thought OK, but while she's talking to me, she looks at my feet, because my shoes are not proper, well they were a little old, and she just says "OK, we'll call you" and all of a sudden they hired this other person. So I thought, "Jeez, I guess it was my shoes." What else am I supposed to think? She didn't say as much as that, but I'm thinking my shoes were important 'cause that's all she was staring at.

She has experienced this discrimination from other employers also. This manifests itself in employers saying there is employment available, and then changing their minds when Melissa arrives in person.

If you do it by phone a lot of them would say "Yes, we're hiring," but if you get there in person they would kind of change their mind type of thing.

Melissa has also been discriminated against because of her weight (her partner Jack who was interviewed with her also comments on this):

Melissa: I really do want to work, but people look at me from head to toe, and people who look at you from head to toe over and over again you know there's something wrong

Jack: They say "The position has been filled" and you go the next day or a couple of weeks later and it says "help wanted." But when you go there they say "No, the position has been filled."

The weight-based discrimination that Melissa experienced was not just from potential employers; she also encountered discrimination from her Ontario Works social worker.

I've been told by one of the social workers here in this office that I shouldn't be working behind a counter. One of the workers — social assistance workers — told me this and I looked at her and I said "Why?" "Well with your weight and whatever you can cause a lot of accidents, people can get burned, blah, blah, blah." Well, that's not encouraging your clients: that's discouraging them from working. And how many people do you have in different offices that will do that? And then you're being penalized

> because nobody knows what these people are doing. Like I mean I was furious when she told me that: I was like "What?"

Melissa is frustrated with this situation because she wants to work for wages; she just has not been given the chance.

> I didn't choose to be on Ontario Works at all. I'm willing to work; it's just nobody wants to give me a chance because of what I look like.

Jane has experienced discrimination partly because of her age and partly because she has been unable to find employment with job security.

> And here I am. I've worked, I've had jobs galore. But jobs don't last. And everybody's looking for younger [people]. And small businesses, people try, like the government and everybody says open your own small business and the government will help you. And what do you end up with after that? You get a nice big bill, because your business does not last because you're in competition with bigger businesses. Like this last job I had, it was a furnace company and air conditioning... And like it was a small business; it went under. I worked there three years and I'd still be working there if the business didn't fold.

Another barrier that keeps people on social assistance is the fact that many low-paid or part-time jobs do not provide health benefits for employees. This is especially difficult for parents, because they need to ensure that they are able to provide care for their children.

> Jane: So the thing is, once you're on welfare, it is almost impossible to get off. And the thing is too, especially when you have children, the jobs that we can get they don't usually cover benefits. And with kids you need to have benefits. So it's like, do I take a job and get paid, so I can have respect again, or do I stay on it [social assistance] and make sure my kids are healthy all the time. Make sure she's got her teeth checked, her eyes. So it's like a never-ending situation. They push and push you to go out and get a job, but they don't think that we need these other things as well. It sucks, once you're stuck on it it's like you're stuck.

Three of the participants reported some relationship between their becoming parents and their ending up on assistance, which highlights the lack of social support for raising children. Jane mentioned that she was not able to get a job because she was pregnant and "showing" while she was on unemployment. Once her unemployment insurance ended, she had "no choice" but to go on welfare. Jack and Melissa's experience with welfare also started after the birth of their first child:

> Melissa: Well it [our experience with welfare] all started about twelve years ago, when we, I got pregnant for my first child. After I got him I was forced to leave the workforce basically.

With Jack working part-time and limited employment prospects for the two of them, social assistance was necessary to survive.

Jane fears what might happen to her son, as he is expecting a child soon.

> You get benefits on welfare and it helps so much. It's the one thing you're afraid to give up. Like my son right now, his girlfriend is pregnant and they're working, well he's working, she had to quit because she has morning sickness, well all day sickness actually. So she can't work but he makes enough to support both of them but now the medical bills are coming in. The company he works for does not offer benefits, so therefore he has to get his own benefits. And I told him he better hurry, to have a baby costs quite a bit.

PROBLEMS SPECIFIC TO RAISING CHILDREN ON ASSISTANCE

During my interviews with the research participants, it became clear that raising children on assistance is hard. Furthermore, as these children approach adulthood, they find it difficult to escape the circumstances in which they grew up, thus creating a cycle whereby the children of social assistance recipients are relegated to the lower rungs of the class hierarchy, both in schools and communities.

All the parents I spoke with hoped their children would not end up on welfare like they did. Jane tells us about raising children on welfare and watching them be disappointed.

> It's hard bringing up kids on welfare. You know the kids see their friends that have parents that work; they get to get involved in a lot of things, take trips — and well, you're stuck. Like my daughter, when she was younger

she wanted to get into karate, there was no money. Now she's into dance at school, and she'd like to get into dancing classes outside of the school, there's no money. Clothes, you're lucky if you've got GST, that you have extra cash on it. Like we have no cable here, we have the internet, but as far as cable on the TV? Can't afford it. For both it would cost about $90. So, you go without a lot. And the hardest thing is to watch your child being disappointed, but there's nothing you can do.

As Jane's excerpt shows, her daughter is socially excluded from participating in certain kinds of activities because her mother relies on social assistance to survive. This is something Melissa mentioned as well:

A lot of times the kids want what other kids do have, but they're not, those other kids' parents, are not on Ontario Works and we are, and we try to explain to them. "You know I wish I could do this for you but we can't. We're limited in money and we can't afford it."

Social assistance does not even provide a sufficient income to purchase the necessities to ensure a decent standard of living, and therefore families are excluded from participation in certain social activities (both in the community and at school). Jane also tells us how this has become worse now that schools have started downloading some costs onto parents.

Like even high school they start charging you. They want books and you gotta pay for everything yourself. Like some of these classes that they offer you. Every high school has their own special class and [high schools name] is theatre arts, dance and theatre arts. And to major in dance, you gotta pay for your uniforms, you gotta pay for your workshop, and you gotta pay for everything. Like you know, just to major in it. It's ridiculous.

But this is not the type of life that people want for their children. Jane is trying to teach her kids so they can learn from her experience.

And all these people that have jobs are all saying get a job, get a job, but we screwed up a long time ago so we're still screwed now. And I'm trying to teach my kids, don't drop out of school because once you do your life is over, because getting on welfare, there's no way off.

This is something that was evident in Jack and Melissa's interview also.

Melissa: It [our experience on Ontario Works] gave us a heads up. Especially for raising children. You know, you just don't... you want them to learn out of what's going on. You just don't want them to go through what you're living so it's kind of open the door to say "Hey, you gotta keep going to school. Gotta keep doing this or else this is what's going to happen and this is how your life's going to be."

They worry about the message that their children have received from their experience. This is part of their motivation for relocating.

Jack: It's not a good example for the kids. 'Cause they'll grow up and say well it's fun to live on that [social assistance] but it's not.

Melissa: And they [our children] think there's no work attached to it. 'Cause my oldest said "I was thinking of going on that [social assistance]," and I said "I don't think so." He said "Well you've been there since I was born until now," but I said "yeah but I have no choice. If I could make it differently, I would but I can't," and he's now talking about going on it.

Jack: So that's why we're doing that big step. To show them you know it's not ok to live on that.

Unfortunately, as Jane told us previously, with the way social assistance is set up now, it is very hard for the children of Ontario Works recipients to become financially independent and improve their standard of living. And with the cost of higher education, it is difficult to imagine how she can afford this for her children.

It's bad enough I got to figure out how to come up with the money for her [my daughter] to go to school, but to afford everything like campus living and everything? It's ridiculous. And the price of books now and tuition fees. Like, my son wanted to be a doctor. We had figured out how much it was going to cost, it was a little over $30,000 and then Harris stepped in. And then it went from a little over $30,000 to over $80,000 it was gonna cost. Books, the internship, everything. Like what the hell? You know you're signing your life away when you ask for a loan.

Not only do state regulations through the Ontario Works program make it difficult for the children of people receiving social assistance to improve their standard of living, but as Jane tells us, careers such as those in medicine, which usually guarantee a very decent salary, are that much further out of reach for their children because it costs even more than it used to to obtain the credentials for these jobs. Despite the fact that there are people who would like to enter these careers, such as Jane's son, the province of Ontario has a severe shortage of doctors.

Even though parents do not want their children to end up in the same situation as them, some of their children already have. One of Louise's daughters is now on assistance, and she faces a situation much like her mother; she has three children she cares for on her own and she is struggling to get by.

> And the worst part is, my daughter is in [city] right now, she has two children that are on a special disability and she has another child that's gonna be on it also. And she's on Workfare... She really doesn't have any money, and her credit card, she got a credit card, maxed totally out because there's, she doesn't want to live in the projects. Because she was — and then when she saw guns and knives, that was it. It's hard.

This also speaks to how the class location of people on social assistance is socially organized through state regulation. As Louise states, her daughter's social assistance benefits are insufficient for her to afford to live in a safe neighbourhood. She was forced to live in the projects, where her family was exposed to violence, and in order to escape this situation she has to rely on borrowing money from her credit cards.

SUMMARY

The social assistance recipients who participated in my research demonstrated that they face a number of social barriers to getting off social assistance. The research participants have also shown me that the Ontario Works program creates a number of problems in their everyday lives and that raising kids on social assistance is difficult. The problems that emerge for social assistance recipients are occurring because the Ontario Works program does nothing to address the social relations that push people onto social assistance (such as lack of jobs that provide a living wage, lack of available full-time employment, limited access to formal education, limited work experience and discrimination).

NOTE

1. In March 2005, 36 percent of Ontario Works cases were single parents, while 9 percent of cases were couples with dependent children. This represents close to half (45 percent) of all Ontario Works cases that are involved in the socially necessary work of raising children (Human Resources and Social Development Canada, 2006).

Chapter 3

ENFORCING WORK NORMS

This chapter discusses how the Ontario Works program enforces work norms. Through an exploration of the problems experienced in the everyday lives of social assistance recipients and using insights gained from Piven and Cloward (1993), I show how the Ontario Works program enforces work norms by creating administrative obstacles that make it difficult for people to stay on social assistance, by providing a lesson for low wage workers and by increasing pressure on social assistance recipients to work for low wages.

ADMINISTRATIVE OBSTACLES

According to Piven and Cloward (1993: 149–61), welfare officials use a number of administrative practices to keep the number of people on social assistance down. When there are too many people on social assistance, welfare is seen as too "generous" and thus encourages people not to work for wages. These administrative obstacles to social assistance include the following: not publicizing the availability of aid or actively seeking out potential welfare recipients; numerous administrative steps in the admission procedure; and requiring a number of documents to prove that a person is in financial need. The numerous steps in the application increase the risk that a person may be denied benefits during the process, and the numerous verification requirements once assistance is granted also bring the constant risk that a person's benefits could be terminated. These practices combined serve to disqualify certain applicants and to discourage some people from applying. The social assistance recipients with whom I spoke, and the relevant program documents I reviewed, gave clear examples of how the Ontario Works program achieves this.

The many steps that social assistance recipients are required to take in order to apply for and maintain their benefits, and to ensure that they continuously prove themselves morally deserving of aid, impose a large amount of unpaid work on social assistance recipients. Accordingly, accessing social services should be seen as a social process, and there needs to be a focus "on the human effort and activity that go into accessing social services" (Mykhalovskiy and Smith 1994: 1). I explore this under the heading of administrative obstacles because all this work is built into the administration of the Ontario Works program and creates obstacles for people accessing social assistance and/or maintaining their "eligibility" for benefits.

Some of these administrative obstacles are contained within the Policy Directives. For example, the Ontario Works Policy Directives lists the following information that may be "necessary to determine and verify the applicant's eligibility for basic financial assistance":

1. The person's social insurance number.
2. The person's health number under the Health Insurance Act.
3. Proof of the person's identity and of his or her birth date.
4. Information with respect to the person's income and assets.
5. A report of an approved health professional relevant to a determination respecting assistance.
6. Information with respect to the benefit unit's budgetary requirements.
7. Information with respect to the person's attendance and progress in an education or training program.
8. Information with respect to the person's employment and proposed employment assistance activities.
9. Information with respect to the person's status in Canada. (Ontario Works Policy Directive 2008: 8.0)

The directive also stipulates that this information may be required for any members of the family applying for social assistance. The task of assembling all this information can obviously be very daunting, and people's ability to do this will differ considerably. This process deters some people from applying, but it also limits who is eligible for assistance.

If a person is unable to produce any of these "proofs," they may be determined to be "ineligible" for benefits. Additionally, a number of people are automatically excluded because they do not meet the requirements around "status" in Canada, and therefore do not get included as "citizens." After complying with all these requirements, there is no guarantee that the person will be eligible for assistance.

The documentary requirements imposed on social assistance recipients through Ontario Works serve to highlight part of the unpaid work required in order for people simply to apply for assistance. There are, however, several other ways in which unpaid work is required from social assistance recipients, and these are related to the ongoing provision of information, as well as participation in "employment assistance activities."

The Ontario Works legislation outlines the following two roles and responsibilities for Ontario Works participants: "provide information verifying initial and ongoing eligibility for financial assistance, including participation in approved employment assistance activities" (Ontario Works Policy Directive 2008: 1.0-9). Both these requirements impose unpaid work on social assistance recipients, and as Margaret explains, these requirements can on occasion conflict, and it can be difficult to determine which is the priority. In her experience, the priority is doing whatever the Ontario Works case worker tells her to do:

> Well one thing that I didn't like, was when the [Ontario Works] worker wanted to see you, they send out these threatening letters, I always thought of them as threatening because at the bottom of the letter it always said "any failure to come in to this meeting at this time would mean that your cheque would be suspended." And so it gave you the impression that you couldn't phone and say, "Well I'm scheduled to do a workshop as part of my placement and you want me in your office at 2:15 on a certain date." "Oh, yeah. I have to meet with you, you have to come in and sign papers." So they want you out there working or doing this placement, but their priority, or your priority they think it's supposed to be dropping everything when they call.

Margaret's example illustrates a number of key issues related to the administration and operation of the Ontario Works program. First, it reiterates this notion that people on social assistance are not doing anything, and therefore Ontario Works regulations mandate work for them to do in order to ensure they continue to receive their benefits (e.g., meeting with their workers whenever they are told to, with little advance notice). Second, the example highlights the power differential that exists between recipients and Ontario Works case workers. Clearly, these two parties do not enter this relationship as equals, and this is evidenced in the ability to threaten to suspend benefits (which can be made on a moral basis; for more on this see Little 1998 and 2003). Participants are at the mercy of Ontario Works case workers because of the power they have over them within the framework of the regulations. Social assistance recipients see their own priority as providing necessities such as shelter and food for themselves and their families, but their priorities can get shifted to whatever their worker requires.

In addition to the "ongoing provision of information," social assistance recipients are also required to participate in "employment assistance activities." These activities are probably the easiest to see as unpaid work, because for the most part they consist of participating in community and employment placement programs. The institutional rationale for these placements is that social assistance recipients are "earning" their welfare benefits in exchange for the work they do.

One of the largest problems here is that assistance is now contingent on participating in employment activities, whereas assistance used to be based solely on need. This serves as an administrative hurdle for some recipients, because if they are unable to comply with this regulation, they can become ineligible for assistance. By adding this condition to the requirements, people can now be disqualified from social assistance despite financial need. When I spoke with Jane about how she got involved in her placement, she told me that the alternative would be getting "kicked off welfare."

> Interviewer: And was it decided by you and the case worker that you would go on a placement?
>
> Jane: It was either take a placement, volunteer or get kicked off.

The work that is done as part of these placements is often performed in addition to domestic/reproductive work and in some cases part-time jobs[1] and volunteering (types of work that are undervalued by the neo-liberal ideology). In December 2007, a total of 79,535 Ontario Works participants with children living at home were required to participate in "employment assistance activities" in order to maintain their benefits. For many of these participants, their youngest child was under five years of age (38,087, or 48 percent) or between the ages of six and twelve (23,311, or 29 percent) (Ministry of Community and Social Services 2008).

One aspect of participation in placement programs that often goes unacknowledged is the actual work that goes into obtaining and maintaining a placement. Despite the seemingly simple characterization of "getting a placement," the research participants told me about the work that goes into achieving this. For most recipients, a placement is obtained through a broker. There are two ways for clients to end up at the broker agency; they will either be referred there by their Ontario Works case worker (delivery agent) or they will come to the agency on their own looking for employment and be referred to a broker when it is discovered that they are in receipt of Ontario Works. Either way, the recipient is required to perform the task of going to the broker agency to make arrangements for a placement, and often the broker agencies are located separately from the delivery agents, which means that these people with very limited resources must travel to at least two different locations.

According to the brokers I talked to, approximately half of the clients are referred to the program through their Ontario Works case workers and the other half come in on their own because they want to find paid work. In order to proceed into a placement program, the recipient must have the permission of their Ontario Works case worker. This requirement may seem odd but this is how the program operates. One would assume that having a social assistance recipient want to work would be a good thing, but there are decisions around funding that come into play when deciding whether or not a person should take on a placement.

Jane explains the additional work that a social assistance recipient must do after being referred to the broker agency.

> Well first of all you go to your worker, get a referral from your worker to the [broker agency], and then when you meet with someone there that does placements, her name is [broker name]. And then she takes your résumé, makes sure your résumé is all up to date, and then she'll discuss what kind of placements you wanna do; then she puts out her feelers and finds someplace. And then you have to go through your police checks and all this other stuff and then you got to go for a job interview. And [broker

name] goes with you, and we both talk to the employer and they decide
if they're going to hire you or not.

Clearly, as evidenced by the detailed description from Jane, a lot of work
is required on the part of a social assistance recipient in order to obtain
a placement. The extent to which some of this work is actually necessary
can be questioned (e.g., police check), but this serves to highlight the
extent to which the program goal is actually to enforce work norms by
requiring a good deal of unpaid work. Also, people will have differing
abilities to do this work.

According to brokers, placements can be initiated in one of two
ways. A participating organization may contact the broker agency with
a placement need and the placement would then be advertised at the
broker agency. Available placements are posted in a central area where
Ontario Works recipients can browse through them. If there is a post-
ing that interests them, they would notify their broker and the broker
would conduct a "pre-screening." The other way for placements to be
initiated is through direct contact by the broker with employers. The
broker agency has a large bank of participating organizations on file,
and brokers may contact one of these agencies if they have a client
that would be a "good placement." The social assistance recipients I
spoke with also highlighted a third way that placements can be initiated
and these were self-initiated by the recipients. For instance, Louise and
Margaret had placements established with organizations for which they
were already volunteering.

Jane mentioned above that the broker discusses the type of placement that a social assistance recipient wants, and this is accomplished
through what brokers refer to as the "intake process." According to the
brokers, the intake interview consists of screening individuals and determining what their interests are, what skills they would like to gain and
what barriers they face. Figure 3.1 is the form that is used to complete
the intake process. Note that the areas mentioned by the brokers are
not explicitly listed on the form. This form is completed by the broker
and serves as a sort of interview guide during the initial meeting with
recipients. I do not know how much information from the intake process
is actually shared with the potential employers.

The intake form highlights how the process for Ontario Works
recipients is more invasive than the regular intake process for employ-

Figure 3.1 Ontario Works Assessment Report

Name: _____	Bilingual: Y N
Drivers Licence: Y N class _____ Vehicle: Y N	Clean abstract: Y N

Number of Children _____   Age of Children: _____
Daycare Required: Y N   Formal / Informal

Type of Employment/Volunteer Experience Seeking:

Most Recent Attachment to the Workforce and the Outcome:

Education & Training:
Highest Grade Completed: _____
Diploma / Equivalency or Certificates

Criminal Record: Y N	Charges Pending: Y N
	CPIC Available: Y N (CH/CP only)
Details:	Date applied for: _____

Special Needs / Health Concerns: Y N
Details:

Additional Comments/Concerns: _____

ment. For instance, some of these questions would not be asked during a regular employment interview as they could be a basis for discrimination (e.g., number of children or special needs/health concerns). Also, before obtaining a placement it is mandatory to undergo a criminal reference check, for which Ontario Works covers the cost. This is yet another invasion of privacy as few jobs would require this type of check (and this is also based on the assumption that recipients could be criminals). Also, questions about whether the person has a vehicle or a driver's licence would only be required for specific types of employment and therefore do not need to be asked of everyone. The section, "most recent attachment to the workforce and the outcome" overlooks experience gained outside of paid employment and can also orient away from the actual interests of the Ontario Works recipient. This entire process is part of the Ontario Works administrative obstacles because it could deter a number of people.

The form shows the invasion of privacy that people on social assistance are regularly subjected to, and this is built into the process of obtaining a placement, because all recipients must complete an intake interview to obtain a placement. This brings into question the extent to which protecting the dignity of participants is actually a priority within the program. Margaret talked about how she was treated at the welfare office, and she points out that, in her opinion, some of how the program is set up and how people are treated is meant to "demean" welfare recipients.

Margaret: Have you ever been to their [the Ontario Works] office?

Interviewer: I have. And I have to say I was very intrigued by all the numbered doors.

Margaret: Oh, yeah. It's like, pick a door. I know, a couple of experiences I've had there, when you go there, you're treated like... a number maybe? I remember going there, I had an appointment — 10 to 2 — I walked in at a quarter to 2, and I walked up to the desk and told them, well I yelled through their bullet proof glass [which separates the receptionist from the welfare recipients] that I had an appointment at 10 to 2 and to let her know that I was here and she goes "Do you have a number?" "No, I have an appointment at 10 to 2," and she goes "I'm not talking to you until you have a number." So I went and I took a number and I sat down she called their numbers, dealt with them, called my number, I got up to the desk at 5 after 2 and said I have an appointment at 10 to 2 and she said "OK, I'll tell her that you're here." She came back with "you're late," and I said "No, I was here 5 minutes before my appointment and you told me to go get a number, remember?" So she says, "well she says you're late now, so you'll just have to wait for her." I went and sat down and thought why would they have appointments if we still had to take a number? I sat there, got called in behind door 2, and she says "You're late," and I said "No, I was here at a quarter to." She says "Why didn't you tell them at the desk" and I said "I did." Good system? No. Where else would you get treated like that? Why wouldn't she just say "OK, I'll let her know you're here and just have a seat." But no, "I'm not even talking to you, get a number." Hello? What do you have against me? I didn't do anything to you. It could have been anybody, but no because I was at the welfare office I can just be treated like that. Those things, like the bullet proof glass and the security guard[2] who stands there freak me out. I've never seen a fight in there, I've never seen anybody arguing in there, so there's no need for it. It's just set up to demean I guess.

Her experience also highlights some of the additional work she is required to do to maintain her benefits, just to meet with her case worker. The process is not as simple as arriving for an appointment. Rather she must take a number and register with the receptionist, despite having an appointment.

Additional work is also required on the part of social assistance recipients once the placements are established. This work is required by the broker under the guise of "monitoring placements." Under the monitoring of placements, the recipient can be visited without prior notice by the broker to "check on the participant, to see how things are going."

While in the program, participants are required to maintain contact at least once per month with the broker. In some cases, contact will be maintained on a weekly basis; according to the brokers I talked to this will "depend on the circumstances." The contact can be in person, over the telephone, through email or through a site visit at the participant's placement. This further adds to the work that social assistance recipients are required to do.

LESSONS FOR OTHERS

The Ontario Works program also enforces work norms by using social
assistance recipients to serve as "lessons" for people working for wages.
Piven and Cloward argue that this happens because

> market values and market incentives are weakest at the bottom
> of the social order. To buttress weak market controls and en-
> sure the availability of marginal labor, an outcast class — the
> dependent poor — is created by the relief system. This class,
> whose members are of no productive use, is not treated with
> indifference, but with contempt. Its degradation at the hands
> of relief officials serves to celebrate the virtue of all work, and
> deters actual or potential workers from seeking aid. (Piven and
> Cloward 1993: 165)

They further claim that the degradation of welfare recipients is required
because of the socially produced contempt the "general public" holds
for this group (Piven and Cloward 1993: 165–75). The degradation of
social assistance recipients by relief officials sends a message to recipients and potential recipients that if they depend on social assistance for
survival they will be required to undergo certain social practices. In this
sense, the main targets of such practices are not the social assistance
recipients themselves but rather the able-bodied poor who remain in
the labour market.

   Providing a lesson for others is achieved through stigmatization.
Goffman's (1963: 3) work is useful in understanding the concept of
stigma and how it is applied to social assistance recipients. He argues
that society is organized around normative expectations and that stigma
is "an attribute that is deeply discrediting." In this sense stigma signifies
a person who differs from the norm (in terms of identity). In the case of
Ontario Works, society is organized around the norm that people work
for wages, and therefore social assistance recipients are inferior because
they do not. "Normals" view them as inferior and therefore they are
treated poorly, and ideologies (such as that contained in the Common
Sense Revolution) are created to explain their inferiority (Goffman 1963:
5). In the quest to be one of the "normals," people desire to avoid social
assistance because of the stigma and low social status attached to the
group, as well as the poor treatment members of this group receive.

The stigmatization of social assistance recipients on Ontario Works is achieved in a number of ways. First, they are portrayed as morally inferior by the institutional ideology contained within the Common Sense Revolution, which "explains" their "deficiencies" as being tied to individual problems related to motivation and work ethic. Second, they are stigmatized through various practices of the Ontario Works program; these include the formulation of social assistance as a "last resort"; the provision of inadequate levels of benefits; the unfavourable social construction of social assistance recipients; the invasion of privacy they are regularly subjected to; and the type of work they are required to do.

From the institutional standpoint, social assistance should be a person's last resort. This is clearly outlined in the eligibility rules:

> The eligibility rules are designed to ensure that working [for wages] is the first resort for people in financial need, and that people turn to Ontario Works only when all other resources and opportunities have been used. (Ontario Works Policy Directive 2008: 1.0–4)

This moves away from providing assistance in times of need to providing assistance in times of desperation. Thus, social assistance recipients are socially constructed through Ontario Works discourse as having personally failed in all their other attempts to survive. This carries the stigma of personal failure and encourages people working for wages to keep working no matter what the wages and conditions may be.

Another way that waged workers are encouraged to remain in the paid labour market, instead of relying on assistance, is achieved by providing inadequate levels of benefits to social assistance recipients. Despite the fact that a person can supplement their social assistance by participating in a placement program, participants felt that the amount of money they actually received was low for the amount of work they were putting in.

> Jane: You work for your contract, you get less than $100 a month for doing these placements and like yeah the money comes in great, it helps a lot. But how far does your $100 go? It doesn't. It was $120 when I was working, when I was doing placement. And it doesn't lead nowhere, it doesn't help all that much. And then you sit there and think you're doing part-time work, you should be paid for your part-time job.

Had the seventy hours a month been completed in a part-time job at minimum wage ($8 per hour), recipients would have been paid much more than what they received from welfare. Before taxes, a person would have earned $560 a month, compared to the $90 to $120 they receive as a top-up to their regular welfare benefits. However, this feature of the welfare system, known as "less eligibility," maintains that the "standard of living provided by the municipality for its dependent poor must be at a less favourable standard than that which the lowest-paid labourer could earn for himself and his family" (Guest 1997: 38). This ensures that welfare levels are not too high to deter workers from selling their labour power, and it ensures that low wage jobs are appealing to those on social assistance. This is part of the reason why workfare programs such as Ontario Works get described as slavery: the people participating in this program are deprived of certain freedoms, they are subject to harsh conditions and they are forced to work for a pittance.

Social assistance recipients are also stigmatized through how they are socially constructed, both by Ontario Works practices and in official discourse. For instance, the "employment assistance activities," in which they must participate in order to "prepare them for the waged labour market" (which are equated with their needs), constructs them in an unfavourable way. The Policy Directives define "employment assistance" as follows: "Employment assistance helps people to become and stay employed," and it includes the following:

- community participation, i.e. activities that help people to contribute to the community and improve their employability; and
- other employment measures including:
- job search;
- job search support services;
- basic education or job-specific skills training;
- literacy training program;
- employment placement, including supports to self-employment;
- Learning, Earning and Parenting; and
- other measures that may be prescribed in regulations. (Ontario Works Policy Directive 2008: 1.0–3)

The "community participation" component consists of the place-ment programs and the items under "other employment measures" speak to how people on social assistance are socially constructed, as well as their perceived needs. The idea that community participation activities will "help them contribute to their community" is based on the notion that welfare recipients are unproductive and that they are not currently contributing to their communities. The ideas that underlie these directives are that people on assistance need help to find jobs, are uneducated and lack skills, are illiterate, lack employment experience and need help with parenting. Such stigma would certainly deter a person in the waged labour market or anyone from going onto social assistance if they had any other choice.

A number of ways recipients are stigmatized through program practices have already been reviewed, and these include the invasion of social assistance recipients' privacy by Ontario Works case workers and brokers, for example, through the documents required to verify "eligibility" or by requiring them to undergo criminal reference checks in order to obtain placements; the unannounced visits social assistance recipients are routinely subjected to (both in their homes and at their placements) by Ontario Works case workers and/or brokers; and the continuous surveillance they must undergo under the rationale of "verifying eligibility." Another way in which they are stigmatized is by virtue of the type of work they are required to do as part of their place-ments.

The work that has been required as part of Ontario Works place-ments in some cases is physically demanding and dangerous, and people on assistance have no choice but to do it in order to maintain their benefits. For instance, Jill, the single mother of four, was required to clean up city streets of drug paraphernalia and discarded condoms.

> They would have like an organization that they would hire us for two hours, say like myself, and other people. And we'd be about four or five people, and out of each district of [city name], especially in the main central part of the city there, and clean up the streets. Streetwise, park for kids, you know, stuff like that.

She did this for two hours a day, seven days a week, for four years. There was a lack of regard for the consequences that this type of work could have on Jill and her family. If she got sick from this work, her four children could be left without a mother. Due to the dangerous nature of this work, the "crew" was provided with equipment to do their job; however, they were not provided with special training on how to handle the items they were recovering.

> It's very cautious; you have to be very, very careful because of all the disease and the HIV. They provide us with good equipment; we had gloves and pliers, special pliers then the yellow container. We weren't trained, but nobody's, maybe it's not the word, but is stupid or whatever to get close to the needle.

In addition to being dangerous, the work that Jill was required to do as part of her Ontario Works placement was also physically demanding. During the winter, the crew was required to replace needle hunting with shovelling snow for older adults (which is symbolic because older people are seen as the "deserving" poor).

> During the winter, [the organization] well they had something else, shovelling snow for older people. They had a little contract, what they would do, say you, you want your driveway shovelled we go there, we shovel and she gives an amount, $10. We go to another house, whatever, they would call the office and they would put the note and everything and we would know where to go.

The type of work that Jill was required to do speaks to the low value that is attached to Ontario Works recipients. In Jill's case, she and "the crew" were required to perform dangerous work that could have consequences for her health and for her ability to care for her family, and to a certain extent the consequences could have been life threatening. Nevertheless, the social assistance recipients performing this work to maintain their meagre social assistance benefits were not provided with any special training. The low regard that is placed on these people and their lives serves to stigmatize them; from the perspective of state relations, they are at the very low end of the class hierarchy and the social practices that make up the Ontario Works program serve to reinforce that. The lack of regard that is placed on their lives suggests that they are almost considered disposable.

PRESSURE TO WORK FOR LOW WAGES

Work norms are enforced by state relations through the pressure the Ontario Works program puts on social assistance recipients to work for low wages. The ways in which work norms are enforced that have been explored previously in this chapter all serve to put this pressure on social assistance recipients. The administrative obstacles always pose the threat that a person could be classified as "ineligible" and thus required to rely on waged work to survive. The amount of work required to maintain eligibility for social assistance benefits can make low-waged work appealing, partly because it would likely entail less work, but also because people get more money. And, the stigma associated with social assistance certainly does not encourage people to go onto or to stay on benefits. Another way that pressure is exerted on social assistance recipients to work for low wages is through the design of the placement programs.

Despite the stated intent of the policy, most of the placements do not lead to employment. In fact, most participants know this going into the placement, and the not-for-profit organizations that accept people make it clear that the placement will not lead to employment.

> Interviewer: Have any of your placements led to employment?
>
> Margaret: No. And both places tell you — most non-profits tell you — that they don't have a job there for you. But they'll take your energy and the skills; you have to help them reach their goals. But they're not going to hire you; they don't have the funding. And that's why most non-profits take advantage of welfare.

Stella, an administrator from an organization that regularly accepts people on Ontario Works placements, told me there is no chance of the placements leading to employment with that organization because they are mainly volunteer-based:

> Stella: No because the only paid employees here are myself, I'm full-time and [person's name] is part-time. We're a volunteer-based organization and we have 123, I think right now, volunteers. So we have to run with volunteers. It takes about twelve volunteers a day to run the services here at [organization name] and because we're a non-profit charitable organization, of course our budget is limited.

Barbara, who works as an administrator for a not-for-profit agency, thinks that there is no expectation placed on organizations that accept Ontario Works recipients to turn placements into jobs.

> I get a sense that, with Ontario Works you can have a position filled continuously for years on end by people where you have no intentions, no interest in saying that we're going to roll this into a viable position that will be paid by the organization.

Indeed, the program description clearly states that there is no need for the placement to lead to employment. This can be frustrating for participants. When I spoke with Jane, she made it clear that she was tired of doing placements that did not lead anywhere. She wants a job and she realizes that, for her, placements are not the route to employment. She had argued with her worker about this.

> Yeah it [the disagreement] was to get a job. I wanted a placement that would lead to full-time job and that's the argument that I had with her because I was tired of doing placements that didn't lead to anything.

According to Jane, the way the placement system is set up assumes the participant will get a job once the placement ends.

> When you're given this placement, it is assumed... that the placement will turn into a full-time job. So therefore, when the contract ends and the placement doesn't continue into a full-time job, they do not give you another placement, okay. Because at this point you're supposed to be working. So because of the placement, the type of placement you normally get, you're lucky, you're one out of a billion people that will get lucky and get a placement that will lead to a full-time job.

Because placements often end without leading to employment, people remain on assistance but are no longer entitled to the additional money they had been receiving through their placements, despite their willingness to continue on with the placements. This is unfortunate because recipients often cited the most common benefit arising from their placement was the extra money it provided on their monthly assistance cheque.

> Margaret: How [has the community placement been beneficial]? It gave us back some of the money that they took when they did the cuts [the

cuts to the level of benefits introduced under the Harris government].
The $105 was like, I had to make that sacrifice and do those placement
hours in order to regain the money that I lost when they made the cutback
because nothing else came down; food costs didn't come down. So I was
now $105, well I got some of that back, if you can say that. That's the
only way it benefitted me.

Undoubtedly when the placement ends and the extra money stops
coming in, it places added pressure on the people receiving social assistance to go out and accept low wage work. For the period of time
when they are on a placement, they become accustomed to the extra
money, and when it stops, the alternative of a low wage job becomes
increasingly appealing.

Jane told me of another person she met, through one of her placements, who was "kicked off welfare" and forced into a low wage job.
She also told me that she was able to get some leniency at the end of
her placement because she is a mother (and thus qualifies as slightly
more "deserving").

> The woman that I was working with at [name of placement organization],
> when I first started there, her contract was extended quite a few times.
> She was there over two years. And then they told her they weren't extend-
> ing her contract anymore. That it was time for her to get a full-time job.
> Kicked off welfare. She ended up working at [a donut shop]. And I mean
> that's about what they do. Because I had a child, they didn't kick me off
> welfare, but what I had to do was start looking for a full-time job.

Jane's experience clearly shows how the pressure to secure employment
is applied at the end of the placement. As evidenced by the situation of
her co-worker, the point is just to get a paying job; there is no criterion
that it be stable, safe or provide a living wage and health benefits.

Another way that the design of the placement program puts pressure on recipients to work for wages is through their time-limited nature.
Despite the fact that recipients may enjoy being able to give their time to
community organizations and may wish to continue, volunteering can
only be done for a limited time. Melissa explains this in further detail:

> The way that [the community placement] worked is you had to do one
> placement for six months, only once in whatever you wanted to do, you

couldn't go back twice, unless you went back under another title. So, basically it was one chance for every place you wanted to be at, but not everybody wanted us. But the people that did want us, you couldn't go back a second, third, fourth time because they were enjoying your work. They were telling us "no you can't unless you find another title." I found that wasn't fair because I could have been working two, three years as a volunteer still, but at least I would have been giving my time to somebody who really wanted me, instead of looking for something that nobody was interested in, you know.

Melissa's experience brings into question the extent to which the Ontario Works program actually aims to help people secure employment by providing them with experience through these types of placements. If the goal of the program was to provide work experience, then why are the placements done for a limited period? Clearly, placements were done for limited time periods because this puts pressure on the recipient to find a low paying job in the waged labour market at the end of a placement.

SUMMARY

The Ontario Works program enforces work norms in a number of ways, which include requiring a good deal of unpaid work and creating administrative obstacles for social assistance recipients to continue receiving benefits. The work required from the recipients who participated in my research in order to apply for, obtain and maintain social assistance was done in addition to domestic and reproductive work, and often part-time and volunteer jobs. The time required to do all this work is probably close to the equivalent of a full-time job. This work also highlighted the extent to which people on social assistance are subject to surveillance and invasion of privacy, all under the guise of ensuring "eligibility" for social assistance.

The Ontario Works program also serves to reinforce work norms in people who work for low wages by deterring them from using social assistance because of the attached stigma. The stigmatization of social assistance and social assistance recipients is achieved in a number of ways and these include presenting social assistance as a last resort, which carries the stigma of personal failure; providing an inadequate level of benefits, all the while requiring recipients to perform work in exchange for their benefits; and socially constructing social assistance recipients unfavourably. The unfavourable depiction is achieved by portraying recipients as though they are not contributing to their communities and suggesting that they need help to find jobs, they are uneducated and illiterate and that they need help with parenting. Program practices, which include invasions of privacy and the physically demanding and dangerous type of work that recipients can be required to do in order to receive benefits, also serve to portray recipients unfavourably.

Work norms are also enforced by the Ontario Works program through the pressure exerted on social assistance recipients to work for low wages. The administrative obstacles to obtaining and maintaining social assistance, as well as the stigma associated with receipt of social assistance, serve to pressure recipients to work for low wages. In addition, a number of specific features of the placement programs also pressure recipients to work for low wages. These include placements not leading to employment, the time-limited nature of placements and the loss of the much needed extra money once a placement ends.

NOTES

1. In March 2008 approximately 12 percent of Ontario Works cases across the province (24,024 cases) were declaring earnings from working for wages. It is however unknown how many of these people were also required to participate in employment assistance activities in addition to this paid work (personal email communication with an Ontario Works administrator).

2. These may be responses to anti-poverty activism and direct action support work across the province.

Chapter 4

ONTARIO WORKS –
PROGRAM PRIORITIES

This chapter explores who actually benefits from the Ontario Works program and in whose interests the program operates. This is achieved in part by looking at how the program operates from the institutional standpoint, through a critical textual analysis of key documents that form part of the Ontario Works program. These include the Ontario Works Policy Directives, the final report completed by participating organizations at the end of placements, and excerpts from the materials used by the broker agency to promote the placements programs. I also use information that was shared with me by the brokers I interviewed, as well as information from participating organizations.

This chapter reveals the real intent behind the Ontario Works program, which has nothing to do with helping people on social assistance but rather aims to benefit employers and the social relations of capital at the expense of people living in poverty. The program is also an attempt to include other agencies in the moral regulation of social assistance recipients.

ONTARIO WORKS' PURPOSE

The priorities of the Ontario Works program are clearly outlined in the objectives contained in the Policy Directives:

- recognize individual responsibility and promote self-reliance through employment;
- provide temporary financial assistance to those most in need while they meet obligations to become and stay employed;
- effectively serve people needing assistance; and

- be accountable to the taxpayers of Ontario. (Ontario Works Policy Directive 2008: 1.0–3)

The first two points highlight the importance of employment as an outcome of the program. These points are embodiments of the neo-liberal ideology, which assumes that people are responsible for their labour market outcomes and that they have an "obligation to become and stay employed." The terms "individual responsibility" and "self-reliance" serve to downplay the Keynesian view that the state has a role in ensuring the well-being of its citizens through providing limited social benefits. Both these items impose onto participants the priority of attachment to the waged labour force, and in practice, in very low-paying positions.

This is a major change from the earlier version of welfare in the province of Ontario and has the effect of negating the other non-waged work that people on social assistance do, such as parenting. In fact, one of the earliest forms of provincial social assistance that was available to the "deserving poor" came in the form of Mother's Allowance, introduced in 1920, and despite the name, the program was concerned largely with children.[1] In essence, the assistance that mothers received through this program was being dispersed for the service they were providing in raising their children and not necessarily as a form of relief (Blake and Keshen 2006: 60). The Ontario Works program represents a complete reversal of this previous form of assistance by the state, because now child care is seen as a commodity, or something that is purchased, and the priority is for the person to be out doing waged work, which seri-ously undermines the value that a parent brings to child rearing work.

The second objective of the program highlights the fact that assis-tance is supposed to be "temporary." This certainly was not the case for the Ontario Works recipients with whom I spoke. All of them had been on assistance for at least ten years, and some had been on assistance for closer to thirty years. This objective speaks to the need to "get people off the system" by pressuring them to take jobs in the low-waged labour market.[2]

The third objective, to "effectively serve people needing assistance," is the issue I investigate in this chapter, because the people I spoke with highlighted a number of problems they experienced in their everyday lives as a result of the Ontario Works program. This brings into question the extent to which meeting the needs of people on assistance is in fact a priority for this program. For instance, if we look at the types of opportunities for training and educational upgrading that are presented through Ontario Works, we see that they do not provide the opportunities that the people need (for instance, for recipients like Jane, who feels she could benefit from furthering her education). The opportunities that are provided are inadequate, as they are limited to "basic education and job-specific skills training," not a general higher education or specific credentialization. Furthermore, the emphasis for people on the Ontario Works program is employment not education, despite what their actual needs may be.

The last objective of the program highlights the accountability to taxpayers, not necessarily to the people who receive social assistance. The accountability to taxpayers is largely defined on a financial basis and this is most likely a response to the Common Sense Revolution, which promised to make "government work better for the people it serves" (Harris 1995: 2). This rhetoric of accountability to taxpayers is central to neoliberalism and has nothing to do with democracy but instead with a fiscal prioritization of the middle class and wealthy (i.e., not people living in poverty).

BECOMING AND STAYING EMPLOYED

From the standpoint of people on Ontario Works, the solution to getting them off social assistance could in part be getting them a secure job with a living wage that provides medical benefits for their family, at the same time as increasing the availability of safe and affordable housing (some of which could be achieved through access to higher education). This solution is more complex than the goal of the Ontario Works program, which is quite simply for people to "become and stay employed." This further brings into question the extent to which the program actually aims to improve people's situations, as opposed to just forcing them to work for wages.

Although the employment assistance people receive is supposed to help them "become and stay employed," both Melissa and Margaret mentioned problems keeping employment they already had because of the Ontario Works program. Their two examples, discussed in the last chapter, speak to the low value assigned to part-time work under the Ontario Works program. Both Melissa and Margaret are mothers, and somehow they were managing to juggle their mothering work with part-time work. Yet the Ontario Works program — whose main goal purportedly is to get people employment — asked them to quit the jobs they already were doing and to stop providing services they already were contributing to their communities, so that they could participate in other activities, which would supposedly help them gain employment. This certainly does not recognize the efforts that people are putting forth and does not encourage or support them in these efforts.

People's efforts are also undervalued in other ways. The Ontario Works program includes regulations that allow recipients to be employed on a part-time basis, but with a certain percentage of their wages being deducted from their assistance cheques. The amount deducted used to be 25 percent but, as of October 2000, went up to 50 percent. For people like Jack, who have been working on a part-time basis for a long time, this change makes their part-time work essentially useless.

> It's [working part-time] not even worth it. If you find a part-time job like me, like just say in a month I make $900, they take off $450 out of what they usually give us at the end of the month. So it adds up to nothing.

His wife Melissa recognizes that the policy is resulting in the opposite of what it purportedly was designed to achieve. Although it is intended to provide an incentive for people on social assistance to work for wages, it proves to be a disincentive.

> I know they are trying to encourage people into doing what's best and finding work, but chopping the whole half [of the wages], that's the only disagreement I have: that won't encourage them at all.

Clearly, not all placements can be expected to lead directly to employment with the organization for which the placement was done. However, all placements should be expected to "improve the employ-ability" of the Ontario Works recipients who participate in them. Indeed, this has been achieved in some cases, as two of the people I spoke with reported developing new skills or improving existing skills through their placements.

> Margaret: Yeah. Hone up on the skills I already had, and develop them further. I guess because I was only there volunteering one day a week

and then it moved up to five days a week every month that I had more time to do what I was doing. I got to learn, develop I guess what I was doing further.

Melissa reported that her placements really helped her with her communication skills.

To me it opened a brand new branch for me so that I'm not as bad as I used to be before towards communication and stuff. So for me it opened at least that door.

These two examples aside, there are instances where the degree to which "employability" was increased is questionable. For instance, in Jill's case, getting help with her learning disability, completing high school or even if her placement had given her more appropriate work experience would have been better choices to boost her employability.

DEFINING EMPLOYABILITY

It is important to look at how "employability" is defined under the Ontario Works program. A key document that expresses how this concept is measured is the report that participating organizations must complete at the end of a placement. One of the research participants from a participating organization shared a copy of this document with me, and it is included as figure 4.1. This report was created by the broker agency, and it is completed by a staff member from the participating organization where the placement was done. The report is then submitted to the broker agency and used for statistical reports and program evaluation.

The report takes the standpoint of the participating organization and illustrates the qualities related to work ethic that the program strives to instill into participants. These qualities are included under "employability" and are considered a measure of placement success. The items are all qualities that employers would look for in an employee, including attendance, punctuality, ability to follow instructions, knowledge of duties/work, quality of work, dependability, initiative, ability to work with others, ability to receive feedback and relationship with supervisor. This list clearly demonstrated that the program aims to meet the needs of employers to have "good" disciplined workers,

Figure 4.1 Community Placement Final Report

Participant's Name: _____   Phone #: _____

Participant's Caseworker: _____   Phone #: _____

Community Placement   Contact
Host Organization: _____   Person: _____
Address: _____   Phone #: _____

        street   apt.#

_____   Fax #: _____

        city/town   postal code

Title of position: _____   Start date: _____   End date: _____

Total duration of placement in weeks: _____   Total duration in hours: _____

Describe the training that the participant received during the placement.

_____

_____

_____

_____

_____

Describe the skills that the participant acquired during the placement.

_____

_____

_____

_____

_____

Please rate the participant's performance with regard to the following:

		Satisfactory	Above Satisfactory	Excellent	Needs Improvement
1.	Attendance	☐	☐	☐	☐
2.	Punctuality	☐	☐	☐	☐
3.	Ability to follow instructions	☐	☐	☐	☐
4.	Knowledge of duties/work	☐	☐	☐	☐
5.	Quality of work	☐	☐	☐	☐
6.	Dependability	☐	☐	☐	☐
7.	Initiative	☐	☐	☐	☐
8.	Ability to work with others	☐	☐	☐	☐
9.	Ability to receive feedback	☐	☐	☐	☐
10.	Relationship with supervisor	☐	☐	☐	☐

Please turn over >>>

continued on next page...

Describe any strengths that the participant demonstrated during the placement.

_____
_____
_____
_____

In what areas could the participant improve?

_____
_____
_____
_____

Identify any additional training that you feel would be beneficial for the participant.

_____
_____
_____
_____

Other comments:

_____
_____
_____
_____

I have reviewed the Community Placement Final Report with the participant.

Community placement host
Representative's signature: _____   Date: _____

Participant's signature: _____   Date: _____

all the while enforcing work norms and furthering the larger project of moral regulation.

INDIVIDUALIZING POVERTY

For most of the people I spoke with, these placements and the "employment measures" did not lead to employment. The reason for this seems clear to me: the program does nothing to address the social organization of poverty or the class location of social assistance recipients. This is because, within neoliberal ideology, attention is focused on individuals and not on social and institutional barriers. This ideology constructs poverty as a problem about individual deficiencies and not as a broader social and political issue. This focus also obscures the class conflict at the heart of capitalist relations.

Despite helping Melissa with her communication skills, the employment assistance activities did nothing to prevent her from being discriminated against because of her weight. Placements did not increase the number of available jobs for Jill, Margaret or Jack. And these placements did not provide the highly valued credentials offered through the formal education system that Jane felt she would need to get a job. She explains:

> They [employers] won't hire you because you don't have the experience. And then when you get the experience you can't get hired because you have no certificate.

The program assumes that experience, basic education and literacy will be sufficient to secure employment, when the reality is that these things are often not enough. Samantha, a manager at a not-for-profit organization, told me that the experience gained through community placements with her agency is not enough for a person to find regular employment afterwards. Rather, successful employment has only been achieved when people followed up their placement by pursuing a diploma in the same field of work.

> Many of the people who were coming in to do their volunteer work [as part of their placements], you gotta look at it that way; many took courses afterwards and became employees at [name of organization]. So, we had a lot of success with the program.

Samantha highlights the fact that some people need to further their education in order to gain employment. Yet the Ontario Works program does not address this barrier. On the contrary, regulations clearly stipulate that the program provides only "basic education or job-specific skills training," not a broader education or credentialization (which restricts the types of jobs people can get, if and when they get off welfare).

And for others, like Margaret and Melissa, who already have the education, the Ontario Works program does nothing to increase the number of available jobs. In fact it may reduce the number of available jobs because some organizations can get free labour from the program.

WORK OF THE BROKER AGENCIES

With a better understanding of some of the priorities of the program as they are revealed through the regulations and how it operates, I now turn to the work of the broker agency. This serves to further illustrate how some of these priorities are carried out in the social practices of the Ontario Works program.

Broker agencies are normally existing social service agencies that offer employment assistance activities to members of the community. For instance, a local centre that provides help with résumé writing and job searching could apply to become a broker and deliver these specific activities to Ontario Works participants by tender. Most often, broker agencies are responsible for delivering the employment workshops and assistance, for recruiting employers and organizations to participate in the placement programs and for developing placements and then matching up the placements to participants. In some municipalities, there are numerous organizations contracted as brokers, which adds another layer of complexity to the program. In addition to the regular Ontario Works case worker, some Ontario Works recipients also have to be accountable to a worker from the broker agency.

The broker agency at which the research participants were employed is responsible for the placement programs and employment assistance activities mandated through Ontario Works. To get a better sense of their role in the program I start by looking at the different placement programs and how they are promoted by the broker agency.

PLACEMENT PROGRAMS

The three different types of placement programs that fall under the umbrella of community participation further highlight the priorities of the Ontario Works program.

THE EMPLOYMENT PLACEMENT PROGRAM

The Employment Placement Program aims to place Ontario Works participants with both private employers and not-for-profit organizations. Employers must guarantee a minimum of twenty-eight hours of work per week, and in return they receive subsidies to cover a portion of the wages for the first four months of employment, as well as accident coverage for the participant for the first six months of employment.

According to the brokers, this program is intended to "assist employers with their human resource needs." In other words, the program is not necessarily intended to meet the needs of recipients; rather it is about meeting the needs of employers. In their advertising material, the broker agency highlights the services this program provides to employers:

> We can provide employers with a subsidy of up to $4.00 per hour depending on the training needs of the worker and wages of job
> WSIB or Accident Insurance coverage for up to 6 months

These two items illustrate how this program subsidizes certain employers and agencies (for an example, see the discussion about the call centre in Sudbury in the next chapter). The program not only subsidizes part of the worker's wages, but it also saves the employer additional costs by covering insurance for a period of time. Since the wages of people on workfare placements can be subsidized for a limited time period when they are placed in for-profit organizations, these workers create more surplus-value because the employer pays these people less than they would if they were regular employees. This is an impetus for hiring people from this pool of candidates for placements. Also, in the not-for-profit sector, where budgets and resources are often very stringent, receiving free labour from people on Ontario Works placements (as well as volunteers in general) is beneficial because their scarce funds can be used in other areas. These factors generate a need and a desire for workfare programs, like the Ontario Works program, both within the not-for-profit and the for-profit sectors.

Furthermore, the fact that welfare programs must cover all these costs in order for social assistance recipients to participate in placements indicates that workfare relief arrangements, such as the Ontario Works program, are much more costly than regular relief arrangements (Piven and Cloward 1993: 383).

The participants provided examples of the types of placements that had been offered to them:

> Jane: She [the broker] wanted to put me on another [placement] list... the things that she wanted to put me on was like that Molly cleaning company, things like that. I mean I didn't want to do that kind of stuff.

> Margaret: I went to her [the broker] and she kind of laughed at me and said "Well, no. We have warehouse work, we have McDonald's, we have dishwashing work, labour work, cleaning rooms in hotels." She said "we don't have anything that would meet your qualifications."

In addition to being placed in these types of service jobs, participants are also being placed with not-for-profit organizations. A number of participating organizations with whom I spoke worked with people living in poverty, and as such they struggled with their decision to participate in this program, because many organizations felt it was unjust to people living in poverty (this is examined in further detail in the next chapter).

In order to be eligible for this program, employers must meet the following criteria:

> Employers may be from Private Sector, Non-Profit Organizations or Government Agencies.
> All employers must have Third Party Liability of not less than 2 million dollars,
> Employers must provide a minimum of 28 hours of work per week,
> Employers must not replace laid off workers or those subject to recall.

None of the Ontario Works recipients with whom I spoke had participated in the "employment placement" stream of the program. They had either been placed in the Community Placement Program or the Community Helper Program. One of the participants indicated there were fewer employment placements because these are costlier to administer.

THE COMMUNITY PLACEMENT PROGRAM

The Community Placement Program is described by the broker agency in their advertising material as follows:

> The Community Placement Program is intended to place individuals who are on Social Assistance in a work place setting with a non-profit or charitable organization. It is expected that the participant will gain valuable work experience and skills while contributing to their community. The organization is under no obligation to offer the participant employment upon completion of the placement. Placements are a maximum of 17 hours per week, 70 hours per month and vary in length.

In the advertising materials, the broker agency goes on to describe the eligibility requirements for an organization to participate in this program:

- Must be a non-profit, charitable or broader public sector organization
- Have the expertise, experience, facilities and management to supervise the placement
- Recognize the dignity, worth and confidentiality of the participant
- Offer a meaningful and productive placement
- Offer a safe working environment
- Possess a minimum of 2 million dollars liability insurance if the participants uses the Host's vehicle

Despite the reference to offering a "productive placement" (which emphasizes the notion that people on assistance are unproductive), the way this type of placement is constructed has some beneficial aspects to it. For instance, there appear to be safeguards around ensuring that placements are valuable for participants and that participants are treated with dignity and offered a safe working environment. Notwithstanding how the program is conceptualized on paper, the research participants highlighted instances where these criteria were not met (these are discussed in further detail in the next chapter). Furthermore, the material does not state how this is to be achieved.

COMMUNITY HELPER PROGRAM

The Community Helper Program is described in the advertising material of the broker agency as follows:

> The Community Helper Program provides Ontario Works participants with opportunities to learn new skills, gain work experience and develop a network of employment contacts by volunteering their services to low income seniors in our community and with non-profit community organizations.
>
> Most placements last for three months and participants are able to volunteer for up to seventy hours per month. Financial assistance is available to help cover costs related to transportation and childcare.

The Community Helper Program is a variation of the Community Placement Program. The difference is that the Community Helper Program is designed for those Ontario Works recipients who face "multiple barriers to employment." Although not stated explicitly in the description, implicitly the goal of the program is to help people develop a work ethic and sense of responsibility, not necessarily to provide them valuable work experience or to help them get a job. This program is most clearly linked to moral regulation, as it is intended specifically to develop values based on hard work and diligence, further enforcing work norms.

Through its work in promoting and administering these programs, the broker agency becomes an agent of state regulation by essentially taking on the priorities of the Ontario Works program to the detriment of their clients. The work they do is no longer simply about helping people to find employment. Through their arrangements with the Ontario Works program the broker agency comes to play a role in enforcing work norms and morally regulating people on Ontario Works.

By putting people into placements that do not lead to employment, by overlooking the actual needs of people on social assistance and by focusing their efforts on résumés and hygiene, brokers are pressuring Ontario Works recipients to accept low-wage work.

In speaking with the brokers, the considerations that came into play for determining whether a person was "ready for a placement" and the barriers and challenges that they perceived their clients to be facing were not the same as what came through in my interviews with Ontario Works recipients. Melinda is one of the brokers I interviewed. When I asked her how she determines if a person is ready for a placement, she discussed motivation as the main consideration that comes into play for her decision-making.

> Motivation is the biggest issue when you're trying to find people that are looking for work. And you can't really measure motivation. So, I determine [motivation] by giving them small tasks to do for me, to see how quickly they get back, and how their follow up skills are... I usually, my favourite thing to do, is I usually ask them for a list of five employers where they would like to work at, five employers that have jobs they'd be interested in, because then they actually have to go out and read a paper. It's not a big task, but when they follow through with it, and come back, then it shows some semblance of motivation. But there's really no way to measure it. I just go with my gut, and hope, with my fingers crossed, that the placement lasts.

Melinda's quote highlights how, in the professional discourse within which she operates, "motivation" becomes an ideological category that is used to evaluate a person's moral character and their work initiative and capacities. Despite this claim that motivation is the biggest issue, all three brokers told me that half of their Ontario Works clients come into the broker agency on their own, without being referred by their Ontario Works case worker. For most people, this would certainly count as motivation.

In terms of the barriers brokers perceive their clients as facing, when I asked Melinda about these, they were not the same barriers that participants expressed in their interviews.

> Essentially, how they look, how they dress and how they take care of themselves, is a barrier when you're going in to an interview. So, I'll work

on that first. We have hygiene kits that we can give out, and we talk about it just freely in a way that is not uncomfortable. Then, the résumé, the experience, whether it's updated.

Both quotes from Melinda clearly highlight the extent to which moral and neoliberal ideologies shape her perception of the barriers that people face to employment, and the resulting services that are offered to them. Through her work with the broker agency, she has come to take on the view that people should be employed and that any failure to do so is their own fault, for instance, because of their appearance or supposed lack of motivation. This is in part due to the pathologization of poverty that is present in the professional discourse. Poverty has come to be seen as a disease that needs to be treated. Also her comments around hygiene have moral implications and are another way that people on social assistance are stigmatized.

In essence, through their relationship with the Ontario Works program, these agencies become another vehicle of enforcement and discipline of state regulation (see Ng 1998 for another example of this).[3] The work that is done by the brokers and the broker agency comes to be affected by state regulations. The brokers, who work in organizations with mandates developed to help people find employment, now have their work guided by programs such as Ontario Works. Not only does this mean that considerations such as the Ontario Works budget now come into play, but it also changes how they view these particular clients. The institutional ideology of the Ontario Works program carries ideas organized around recipients as facing individual barriers to employment; they are seen as unemployed not because of systematic or societal forces but because of their own individual faults. This attitude comes to permeate the work done by brokers as they attempt to overcome these so-called barriers to employment, when in fact they often fail to see the actual barriers that people face. The people I spoke with needed help with educational upgrading, with securing health benefits for themselves and their children and with fighting discrimination from employers and case workers. These are not addressed as barriers to employment because of the way welfare recipients are socially constructed in this program. Through the funding arrangement with the Ontario Works program, the broker becomes part of state and moral regulation.

The brokers I talked to showed me that regardless of the intentions of people working in the broker agency, they do not provide Ontario Works recipients with good sustainable employment. Rather they further the project of moral regulation by enforcing work norms, both by pushing people to work in placements and by making them perform a great deal of unpaid work in order to receive their benefits. This has nothing to do with helping people get good jobs or helping them to get off welfare; it has everything to do with exploiting people living in poverty for the benefit of capitalist social relations.

SUMMARY

This chapter has highlighted the extent to which the priorities of the Ontario Works program are to get social assistance recipients out into waged work and to meet the needs of the social relations of capital by providing subsidies to employers and providing an impetus for recipients to go out and accept paid work. The program also morally regulates recipients by instilling values of "hard work" and "diligence." The way the program works does not address the social barriers such as lack of full-time employment, lack of access to higher education, lack of jobs that provide health benefits and discrimination that recipients face. The failure to recognize these social barriers serves to individualize the issue of poverty. Focusing the blame for poverty on individuals results in programs that ignore the social relations that push people into poverty and results in "solutions" that do not address the root causes of the problem of poverty.

The participants have also shown me how, through agreements with broker agencies and participating organizations, state regulations attempt to involve these organizations in the moral regulation of people on social assistance. By involving broker agencies in the administration of the placement programs and the "employment assistance activities," the work that is done by these agencies gets transformed in order to be consistent with the institutional ideology of Ontario Works. As a result, the organization ends up serving the needs of employers and the social relations of capital, at the expense of people on social assistance. This is similar to the transformation of an immigrant women's centre Ng (1998) examined, whereby through the centre's relationship with the state, its work, which had previously been centred around advocacy, changed as the centre came to slot women into low-waged positions.

NOTES

1. The more recent focus on child poverty is another means to divide people into deserving and undeserving poor.

2. The statistics that are available on the duration of assistance do not classify recipients beyond "25 months or more" on assistance, which makes it difficult to determine how long people remain on assistance. This is further complicated by the fact that people can leave social assistance numerous times only to eventually return. Nevertheless, in March 2005, 42 percent of Ontario Works cases had been on social assistance for thirteen months or more, with 24 percent of cases having been on assistance for twenty-five months or more (Human Resources and Social Development Canada 2006).

3. Ng (1998: 13) explored how an employment agency with a mandate to help immigrant women did not only organize, but actually "helped rationalize labour market processes on behalf of the state." Through the state funding arrangement, the organization's work became defined in terms of services to clients and employers, and not as advocacy.

Chapter 5

PROBLEMS FOR
PARTICIPATING ORGANIZATIONS

With a better understanding of the actual priorities of the Ontario Works program as revealed through the work of the brokers, I turn my attention to what can be learned about how the Ontario Works program is socially organized by looking at the experiences of people in participating organizations. In speaking with people from participating organizations, it became clear that the Ontario Works program created a number of problems for this group as well (although these were quite different than the problems created for social assistance recipients). These are examined in further detail here as I explore some of the struggles these organizations faced in their decisions to participate in the Ontario Works program.

STRUGGLES AGAINST WORKFARE

Before discussing some of the problems that organizations faced in deciding whether or not to host Ontario Works placements, it is useful to give a brief overview of some of the struggles that have occurred in relation to workfare. Two specific examples from Sudbury are examined here briefly: the formation and outcome of the Sudbury Works Advisory Committee, and protests against the expansion of workfare into the private sector.

In 1996, shortly after the Ontario Works mandatory workfare requirement was announced, the city of Sudbury[1] formed the Sudbury Works Advisory Committee, a group charged to develop a business plan for how this program could be implemented locally (Gervais 1996). The committee was to have "as many representatives from community groups as possible"; however, representatives from the Sudbury and

District Labour Council refused to get involved because "workfare is inhumane and does nothing to address the real problem of unemployment" (John Filo of the Sudbury and District Labour Council, as quoted in Whitehouse 1996a).

Nevertheless, the eleven-person committee did manage to attract some representatives from community groups, including Bobbie Cascanette from Group Action Against Poverty. However, Cascanette decided to resign from the committee after their second meeting, saying "the committee was a sham and that most of the important decisions have already been made by the DSSSAB [District of Sudbury Social Services Administration Board]" (Whitehouse 1996a). Cascanette announced her resignation from the Sudbury Works Advisory Committee by holding a news conference and staging a chain-gang, organized by Group Action Against Poverty, to draw attention to the situation social assistance recipients faced in light of the upcoming workfare program. Cascanette charged that many of the committee members opposed the mandatory nature of workfare; nevertheless, they were not willing to do anything to challenge it. Administrators from social assistance countered that the program was being mandated by the province and the committee's role was simply to advise on how best to implement the program locally (Gervais 1996).

The Sudbury Works Advisory Committee held a public forum seeking input on where community placements could be created. The group was looking to create over 1,500 placements for the January start date, but of the approximately seventy-five people who showed up at the meeting, only one person came with suggestions for placements. The remainder of community members were there to express their opposition to workfare, including worries that people would be cut off welfare for being unable to comply with the requirements and fears that workfare would displace paying jobs and "exacerbate problems faced by many welfare recipients, such as low self-esteem, mental and emotional problems and lack of effective job training and education" (St. Pierre 1996a).

Critics of workfare raised opposition to the program because it is based on the assumption that people do not want to work. The advisory committee members contended that "there is no point to such a protest [against workfare] because the Conservative government won't be swayed from its commitment to workfare" (St. Pierre 1996b). Advisory committee members expressed frustration that "little was resolved" at the public forum (Whitehouse 1996b). Nevertheless, many community activists would argue the opposite, because shortly after the public forum, the advisory committee made the decision to postpone the local introduction of workfare by one year (a motion that had previously been defeated when proposed by Cascanette) (Whitehouse 1996c).

The example of the Sudbury Works Advisory Committee highlights a number of issues related to the struggles against workfare: first, the lack of participation from community groups on the advisory committee illustrates their opposition to the program. Second, the only anti-poverty activist on the committee felt her voice was not being heard when it came to the advice the committee was providing to the province about the program; she was discounted because her suggestions were not consistent with the professional discourse being promoted from the government. The fact that some committee members indicated their opposition to the workfare program, yet did nothing to challenge it, shows how these people, by giving the program legitimacy and consent, became agents of state regulation. The formation and the outcome of this group also highlights some of the key concerns surrounding workfare — notably that it is inhumane, that the lives of people on social assistance would be made more difficult as a result of this program, that people would be thrown off welfare for failure to satisfy work requirements and that jobs would be displaced by placements.

Another key struggle that emerged regarding workfare surrounded its expansion into the private sector. When the program was initially implemented, only not-for-profit organizations were able to receive community placements. However, on March 15th, 1999, then Minister of Community and Social Services Janet Ecker announced that workfare would be expanding into the private sector (email communication from the Ontario Coalition for Social Justice, March 13, 1999). As a result of this announcement, the Sudbury Coalition for Social Justice held a conference outside where the Minister was making the announcement to express their disagreement with the expansion of the program and to raise awareness surrounding some of their key concerns with the program, notably "how the province's mandatory workfare program forces people on social assistance to work for half the minimum wage," and how it "acts as a strong downward force on all wages, as well as punishing people already living in poverty" (Sudbury Coalition for Social Justice 1999).

The result of this announcement made it increasingly clear how workfare programs, such as Ontario Works, come to meet the needs of capital. After the announcement of the expansion of Ontario Works into the private sector, a Toronto-based company, Omega Direct Response Inc., opened up a call centre in Sudbury, creating 925 new jobs in this location. Two hundred of these jobs were filled by workfare placements, and the company received 1.35 million dollars in subsidies in return for hiring Ontario Works participants (Citizens on the Web – News 1999).

THE DECISION TO PARTICIPATE

In speaking with some of the research participants who had been involved in the early struggles against workfare, it became clear that for some time, there was a pretty unanimous position among anti-poverty activists, unions and social service agencies that workfare was wrong. Workfare was a direct attack on people living in poverty and it was coercive. In fact, Sophie, an administrator from a participating organization, equates the program with slavery (much like Louise did earlier).

> It's [workfare] just now become another criterion that poor people need to go through to get their measly $520 a month. So, you know it's punitive, it's actually quite frightening because it puts, it forces these people to do work, which is a precedent, you know, in our modern Canada... we've introduced a new form of slavery. So, whereas people who cannot find a job, they know they're going to be forced into some kind of labour situation that they don't necessarily want to be in. That's huge, that's an enormous precedent in our country.

This strong opposition was the original position, but eventually discussions began to open up and there began to develop an attitude amongst some of the social agencies that they could actually, in a limited way, protect or help some people living in poverty, who are on Ontario Works, if they accepted them as workfare placements in their organizations.

The majority of people I spoke with in participating organizations represented organizations that worked with people living in poverty. Most of them did not subscribe to the ideologies perpetuated about social assistance recipients within the ruling relations of neoliberalism, and, therefore, many of them were conflicted when faced with the dilemma of whether or not they would host Ontario Works placements. Barbara, who was working for a different organization in 1996, when the program was implemented, explains why that organization would not have taken part in the program:

> There were a lot of discussions on our part about how it was not in, that we were not in favour, it contravened with the principles of fair pay for fair work. In that it wouldn't have been something that that agency would have ever engaged in.

The people within that organization saw the Ontario Works program as "wrong" because it did not provide people receiving social assistance with a fair wage for the work that they were being required to perform. However, when Barbara moved to the organization for which she works now, they were taking on Ontario Works placements, and she put an end to this because it went against the principles of fair pay.

> When I came in, we discontinued our involvement, we discontinued our relationship with Ontario Works, primarily for the reason that we held, that I held before, that it goes against the understanding that people should get paid a fair pay.

In another organization where Ontario Works placements had been created by staff, it created a conflict within the organization because some non-staff members were opposed to the Ontario Works program. Anita explains:

> The staff suddenly had taken on I think it was two — for sure one person on Ontario Works. And this had never been discussed at a collective meeting. It had never been discussed by the board members. And so on the one hand, as volunteers coming to a meeting, we asked "How did this happen?" On the other hand we didn't want to antagonize staff because there was a fair amount of hostility already there between the volunteers and staff. But we insisted that we had to talk about it, because I'd say there were at least three board members and myself particularly concerned, that why were we taking in people on Ontario Works. We felt this way for all the reasons that people have criticized Ontario Works: we didn't want to be complicit in supporting that kind of system.

Danielle explains how conflict arose in another organization because, although they did not want any part in the program because they do not agree with the fundamental notions on which it is based, they were also being approached by some of their existing volunteers who were on Ontario Works, who wanted to complete their placements within their organization. This made the decision to not participate in the program a difficult one.

> It really boiled down to — there was only two main points. One, we were philosophically opposed to this mandatory placement and we couldn't support it and show success for the provincial government in this by doing the placement. And on the other side we had a number of volunteers who would qualify for the program and who would prefer to do their placement with us, because they would be treated more gently than if they did it somewhere else. And that was why it was very, very difficult to come to a conclusion. And the final conclusion was that I was not going to take responsibility either for the placement — I was the main full-time employee at the time, I would have been the one staff-wise signing for them. And I wasn't going to take responsibility for them, or over them.

Danielle's quote shows how the situation of people receiving social assistance became increasingly complicated once the Ontario Works placement programs were implemented. As Danielle tells us, there were a number of people receiving social assistance who were already volunteering for her organization, who would have been eligible to complete their placements within her organization. Because of the organization's opposition to the program, the organization did not want to create placements for them, meaning that these people now had to go out and seek other opportunities to perform work as part of a community placement to maintain their social assistance benefits.

Danielle tells us that another reason the organization decided not to take on participants was because the confines of the program made it hard to make the experience valuable, both for the organization and the participant. Danielle explains:

> Many of the people that would qualify for placement would have a wide range of skill levels, both interpersonal and work skills. So it's a lot of resources for an agency to take them on. Especially for seventeen hours a week for three months you're not getting a lot of valuable work if you're

trying to train them to do anything that's at all complicated. From an agency point of view, they're more valuable if you just get them stuffing envelopes or doing the brainless tasks. But that doesn't do a lot for the people on the placements.

This quote exemplifies certain aspects of the program and how it is organized that make it difficult to actually provide meaningful experiences to these people. Employers are saying that because of the short-term nature of placements, they are better using workfare participants to do low-skill jobs rather than investing in training them to do other tasks. This is because, with the way the program is set up, recipients have no guarantee that they will be able to stay with an organization for a long period of time (thus providing a return on the time invested in training them). The usefulness of the experience provided to people on social assistance is therefore reduced, because it is not in the interest of employers to invest in meaningful training and because providing meaningful training is not what workfare is about.

The decision not to accept Ontario Works participants at that time was seen as risky, mainly because some of these organizations received provincial and municipal funding. Sophie tells us that it was brave for an agency to take this stand:

A lot of, you know, [organization name], for example, gets provincial funding, that's how it survives, right? So, I mean, you know, refusing to take workfare recipients was putting our necks on the line, at that point too. So any provincially funded agency and organization were being very brave at that point, you know, to say no.

Danielle goes on to explain how the pressure to take on placements started to emerge in funding opportunities:

But a lot of, especially, programs and agencies within town that were getting municipal funding in any form were being pressured to take placements. And it was, it would come up in ways that if they put up a proposal for the funding, it was suggested that they could get more manpower [sic][2] if they had placements. And it was pretty commonly understood that if you wanted municipal funding you were going to have to participate. I don't think it was written anywhere, but it was commonly understood.

Despite the fact that this program contravened many of the principles espoused by organizations working with people living in poverty, some organizations decided to accept people on placement because they saw this as an opportunity to help or protect them. Sophie explains how her organization gradually came to take on participants because they saw that they would be hurting social assistance recipients otherwise:

> It was a gradual thing [deciding to accept Ontario Works placements]. I mean at that point, when workfare was implemented and for awhile afterwards, we were, there was a whole group of us who were standing, we're not going to take this. But then when we realized our principles, in this case, were going to be hurting the social assistance recipients, because they were being forced literally to do something, and if we weren't going to take them on, then they were going to be forced to do something probably much worse. So, at that point, yeah, I think for most organizations, that's what's happening. They have their regular volunteers, who literally, "I have to leave, I'm being forced to go, you know, to do this and so these guys aren't taking you know... you're not taking workfare, I'm gonna have to leave or you know, my life is gonna get much more complicated." So, again, I think it was one by one, the different agencies slowly, quietly, started to take them on.

Sophie's quote shows how the lives of people receiving social assistance became increasingly complicated as a result of workfare requirements. The situation of people receiving social assistance put added pressure on organizations to create placements for recipients within their organization, despite the desire of the organizations not to participate in the program. This can in turn create resentment for people in the organizations, serving to further stigmatize social assistance recipients, which is dangerous for how social assistance recipients might be treated.

Anita also details how staff from her organization argued for taking on participants both for humane and pragmatic reasons:

> Essentially they [the staff] were arguing that they could see that some people on Ontario Works, typically they would be, you know, women living in poverty and if they were going to be taken in to any particular agency, they probably would be treated as lesser people and not with respect. They wouldn't develop any real skills, and so weighing things up it was much kinder and more humane to be offering the opportunity for

women to come to the [name of organization], where they would be part of the collective. There would be no sort of hierarchical thing; they would be treated with respect like everybody else. And they would be able to develop skills, because we had annual volunteer training — typically two weekends in a row — where they were, really in years past, it was very good training that volunteers got. And then within the office itself, the possibility of training to eventually do one-on-one counselling or group work, that kind of thing. So, it was from that sort of humane perspective that staff were arguing why they [wanted to take on recipients], plus the fact that they worked and wanted office help with photocopying and answering the phones when they wanted to have their own staff meetings, that sort of thing. So, for pragmatic and humane reasons they wanted them.

These excerpts from my interviews highlight that the program has the capacity to extend its moral regulatory character beyond the walls of the government responsible for its administration. In fact, the community participation aspect of the program is an attempt to include non-governmental organizations in enforcing work norms among welfare recipients. In order for participating organizations to receive people on placements, they must agree to participate in certain activities around supervision and monitoring. It is important to note that the extent to which organizations engaged in this discourse around Ontario Works varies; the important thing is to give the illusion that they are participating in these activities by submitting proper documentation. The research participants showed that this program has forced a number of not-for-profit organizations who work with people living in poverty to compromise their principles in taking on Ontario Works participants. In spite of their disagreement with the program, and the principles underlying it, these organizations were exposed to external pressures that resulted in many of them participating in the program.

Despite the worthy intentions articulated as reasons for taking on Ontario Works placements, Anita goes on to tell us how these did not materialize during placements with her organization.

And from what I recall while the idea was that they could receive the regular kind of volunteer training in an effort to enable them to do front-line work as soon as possible, I don't recall seeing that actually happen. What I do remember happening is, "Could you photocopy this?" "Can you help us get agenda packages ready?" really tedious work. "We're

> having a staff meeting right now and we need somebody to go answer the phones. Could you go and do that?" So — not that answering phones is menial work — but it doesn't involve, or it didn't involve for them anyway, skill development. So I didn't see that initial promise actually happening. But I did see one or two staff members in particular not treating these people with the respect that they claimed they would. They really were treated as sort of peons and sort of servants and lucky to be here, and that kind of attitude, which upset me to no end.

Anita's quote illustrates how, despite having positive intentions, the placement does not necessarily provide a worthwhile opportunity for participants. In the next section I focus on what recipients had to say about their experiences on placement.

EXPERIENCES ON PLACEMENT

The Ontario Works recipients I interviewed told me that their experiences on placement varied from organization to organization. For example, Margaret describes the difference between two organizations in regard to the way they interpreted and applied community placement regulations:

> One organization was very strict and strategic about getting people who were on Ontario Works, like they were just placements and that's what you were treated like — you were just a placement. You had to sign in, you had to come in, you had to phone if you were going to miss a day or be late, because they definitely took notes and made sure that that was reported back in your evaluation. A little more stricter than the other one. [The other organization] didn't really like the idea of workfare but because they knew that they were going to lose their volunteers, when people like me came and asked if they could volunteer here and collect money for the hours they were already doing if it was okay with everybody. And basically I filled out my own hours. I reported to them, there was a slack in the supervision but I still had to give reports on my own. It was all self-motivated and self-directed. A lot more lenient.

The difference in treatment can be seen as relating to the extent to which members of the organization engage with neoliberal ideologies and the constructions of social assistance recipients that fundamentally shape the program. In organizations where the administrators and the staff subscribe to the neoliberal views inherent in the policy, the treatment is "stricter." Where the organization does not subscribe to the neoliberal discourse, there is increased leniency for recipients. The fact that the experience on placement of a person receiving social assistance can vary from one organization to another speaks to the lack of safeguards in place to ensure that meaningful experiences are provided for people on social assistance.

The recipients also spoke more generally about the way they were treated while on placement. When asked how she was treated, Jane replies that although she was treated "pretty good" on placements, there were still some people who treated her as inferior:

> Jane: Usually pretty good. There are some people that treat you with, act like you're below them. Usually I got along with everybody. I might have one or two people who thought they were better than I am but I didn't care. I'm doing my job, that's all that counts. That's all I'm there for; I'm not there to make friends.

Louise also reports an instance of a co-worker being unpleasant with her because of her education and language.

> And then, oh yeah, I had one that kept on telling me, "You shouldn't be here, you don't have [a] degree and your French is not French." It was this guy; oh he was a real pain in the ass... But it was the degree... I had all these jobs, I was doing them. It was just the idea that, we were all paid the same amount. And they couldn't see why a person, who had only their grade twelve, should be paid the same amount as an ex-teacher. These are young ex-teachers.

Margaret describes how in one organization, people were also treated differently based on whether they were regular volunteers or on community placement. She points out that the term "placement" has several connotations. For example, within the criminal justice system, a "community placement" is something a person might be obliged to do as an alternative to imprisonment.

> The other people who were placements there were referred to as placements a number of times and that was confused with community placements, i.e., the justice system. So when you said that this person was a

> placement, it was assumed that this person might be working off jail time, you know, so you weren't always sure. And the placement, the welfare placements knew who was on welfare so when they worked or volunteered together they knew that and they were working with volunteers who never were on welfare so were kind of looked at like they weren't volunteers they were placements, a little lower level than a volunteer.

Margaret gives an example of how in one organization for which she had previously volunteered, her experience changed when she started there "on placement":

> There was a person there that I volunteered with that was middle management. Let's just say that we didn't always see eye to eye, but that I worked with her there and that was fine. And I can hold my own with her. When I started as a placement, she became my supervisor, my superior, and made sure that she was going to record any time that I challenged her and she did on one of my evaluations. She said that I was difficult to work with and needed more skills in certain areas; that only came up with her. You know attitude kind of thing. She took that opportunity because I was a placement, which I don't think she would have when I was a volunteer. But they did, and they knew me very well there; I had been volunteering there for a lot of years, eight to nine years at that point.

The fact that these people were treated poorly while on placement because they are receiving social assistance speaks to their class location within the waged labour market; clearly, in the eyes of some of the administrators of participating organizations and of some of the co-workers in these organizations, people receiving social assistance are seen as inferior.

Sophie, from one of the organizations that accepts Ontario Works placements, tells us however that she does not treat people on placement different than if they were regular volunteers:

> We're talking about volunteers who are volunteering with us anyway. So, for example, one woman is amazing at acrobatics.[3] So, she would help us to organize the youth when we had acrobatics. She would train youth in acrobatics. But, as a volunteer [on Ontario Works], I would treat her the same way I would treat any volunteer. I had no expectations that she was going to do this for us, and this is what she loved to do.

This highlights the fact that experiences can be made better for participants by the organizations that take them on, not only by treating people similarly to other volunteers, but also by realizing the situation in which they are living. For instance, Jane recounts an example where the organization she was doing a placement with helped her out in a time of need because they were cognizant of her situation.

> Like one time they [the organization I was doing my placement with] really helped me out because welfare cut me off. My daughter was just going back to school and they withheld my cheque. They found out that I was living in a house that my brother owned. See family, you're not supposed to be able to pay rent to family, they should just let you live there for nothing. Like they don't have their own bills to pay, they're gonna let their family live there for nothing!? And the result was they [welfare] held my rent for September as well as October. They held my cheque altogether in September and when I came in to work my boss asked me what was going on. And because they had cancelled my contract [community placement], welfare did, and... they didn't notify me. She had to notify me. And I'm like, what? They cancelled my cheque, my daughter's just starting school, I have no food, no nothing. And so they [the organization] set me up. They loaded up my car with groceries, oh my god. They were so good to me. Like I had four big boxes of food that lasted me about two weeks, they were so good to me. That's because too that I was working there; I got along so well with everybody.

The research participants who worked at participating organizations clearly discuss that their decision to participate in the Ontario Works program does not equate to their acceptance of the program. The fact is that for the time being, this program exists and although much work needs to be done to change the program and the way it operates, organizations can offer some protection to Ontario Works participants from the poor treatment they may receive in other settings. The different experiences that people had on placement speak to the lack of safeguards around ensuring that people on social assistance receive positive experiences. These safeguards are lacking because as the research participants have shown, the Ontario Works program has nothing to do with providing positive work experiences or developing skills for people receiving social assistance. The Ontario Works program is simply about pushing people to work for low wages and enforcing work norms.

I also learned that it is not only organizations that have the ability to make the Ontario Works experience somewhat better for participants, but that Ontario Works case workers can also impact the experience, all the while working within the confines of a very prescriptive program (Ontario Works case workers are employees of the municipality and they provide "assistance" directly to social assistance recipients). For instance, Jill tells us how lucky she was to have a good worker who encouraged her:

> Actually if you have a good worker, you know, and I was lucky to have a good worker you know, because some of them they can be nasty, you know. Strict and don't bother, you know what I mean? But I was lucky, I was lucky to have a good worker, supporting me as much as I went through a lot. Not pushing me, but "Good for you Jill."

Jill's experience is completely different than that of Melissa, who reported her worker making remarks that discouraged her from working in certain fields because of her weight.

Another group with the opportunity to influence the experience of Ontario Works recipients are the brokers, for example, by recommending that the placement be extended, providing additional time for the person to remain on placement and receive the additional money. Margaret explains:

> Interviewer: Just going back to something that you said earlier, that your placements had been for a year and a half and two years. Is there a requirement that after six months it needs to become a new position?

> Margaret: Well again, they have it on paper that it is, except that everybody doesn't fit into those little boxes. The first one I did, I think it was nine months or six months and then you can get extended for three months and then after the three months we just phoned them up and said, "Well, I'm not going anywhere and if the placement still needs me can I just stay here?"

It is, however, unfortunate that organizations cannot know beforehand whether the placement will be extended because, as Danielle highlighted earlier, since placements are normally short in duration, it is not in the best interest of the organization to spend time training people to do complex work.

Another example where extensions can be granted beyond the normal program length is for older people, for whom age may be a barrier to employment. Two of the organizations that I spoke with highlighted instances where this was the case:

> Stella: The longest I had someone on placement was two and a half years. And that was the person that was close to retirement. So after the first year they just kind of let her stay and they didn't see the need to be trying to find her another placement since she was sixty-four years old and waiting for her old age pension.

> Samantha: And you know, I think of the elderly, well the older person, so the one that's in her fifties, how many people would re-employ somebody who's fifty? So that's where you would want the extension.

These examples illustrate how the Ontario Works program does not address the actual barriers that people face to employment. For many people, age is a barrier, and making such allowances within the program enables employers to continue to discriminate based on age. Instead of addressing age discrimination in hiring practices, the program allows this barrier to persist. The participants showed me that despite the fact that there is space for relatively arbitrary decisions within the policy regulations, there really are no opportunities to get people out of living in poverty; these decisions can just improve their situation somewhat.

Despite having some ability to influence the experience of participants, there are external factors that must be considered when broker and case workers are making decisions. In the following quote Stella mentions that funding must be considered when it is time to determine whether extensions will be granted.

> Well that becomes, again that's up to the [broker agency]. And usually the Ontario Works worker, the person who's on Ontario Works has a social worker, so it's usually in agreement with them. The [broker agency] would contact that worker and say "okay can this person be extended?" Or the [broker agency] would know maybe they couldn't be because there was no more funding but if there was a chance, it was the person at the [broker agency] that would go to bat for the person that wanted the extension. And usually I would communicate that to the person on placement, to see if they were interested in an extension. And most of the time they were, the odd time they would say "no, I think I need to

> look for something else" because this is maybe not what they are look-
> ing for or they need training in a different area and they're not getting
> enough of that here. So then it would be communicated to the person
> at Ontario Works and they would have the last say. They would decide
> whether the money was there because the cheque would come from
> Ontario Works for that placement each month.

The role of funding in the decision-making process explains some of the
other discrepancies I encountered in speaking with the participants. For
instance, Jane tells me that her broker did not want to put her into secre-
tarial jobs because she had people with more experience in that field:

> I told them [the broker agency] I wanted to do secretarial work, because
> that's the work I was doing, and she told me that she has one woman
> there that was a secretary for seven years and so she's not gonna put me
> on that list. She wanted to put me on another list and I told her I wasn't
> interested in other things.

Meanwhile, in speaking with Stella about recruiting people to participate in placements, she recounted that the hardest position to recruit
for was that of office worker.

> Interviewer: And did you often get multiple people applying for your
> [community placement] postings?
>
> Stella: No, we got what we needed. If I was looking for maybe two in the
> [specific area] then chances are I got one for sure and maybe had to wait
> for the second one. The one that took the longest to find sometimes was
> an office person. It was always harder to find somebody with appropriate
> office skills or just the right match for this place as well.

It is unjust for case workers and brokers to have the discretion to
make decisions that affect the experiences of people receiving social
assistance. However, from an institutional perspective, the power that
these groups have over social assistance recipients is seen as justified
because the relationship between these groups has been professionalized
as one between a practitioner and a client. But, the truth of the matter
is that the relationship is one of exploitation, where the practitioner
indirectly exploits social assistance recipients who are living in poverty
for the benefit of others.

SUMMARY

Clearly, from an organization's standpoint, the decision to participate in the Ontario Works program can be a difficult one. As we saw from the early struggles against workfare, a number of organizations opposed the program because they saw it as being inhumane. Despite this opposition, over time a number of organizations came to participate in the program, and the people I spoke with from participating organizations demonstrated how, through various requirements for the placement programs, state relations attempt to involve them in its project of moral regulation. They also highlighted a number of problems with practices in the Ontario Works program, notably a lack of safeguards around ensuring valuable and safe placements, and employers being discouraged from investing in training for recipients because of the short-term nature of placements.

NOTES

1. This was before the amalgamation to the "City of Greater Sudbury."
2. This is a sexist term and could be replaced by staff or labour power.
3. The activity has been replaced with "acrobatics" to maintain confidentiality.

Chapter 6

MEETING THE NEEDS OF
SOCIAL ASSISTANCE RECIPIENTS

This final chapter discusses some of the main findings from the research and examines the main contributions it makes. I highlight the implications of this study as they relate to the lives of social assistance recipients, social assistance and workfare programs. Recommendations for change are also provided.

THE SOCIAL ORGANIZATION OF ONTARIO WORKS

Figure 6.1 presents a map of the social relations that socially organize the Ontario Works program. The map highlights the extent to which the state is connected to the capitalist organization of society. Far from being an arbiter mediating conflict between classes and protecting individual rights of workers, in the case of Ontario Works, state relations operate in the interests of capital. Concurrent with Renaud's (1975) argument, capitalism creates the problems of poverty and unemployment and state relations create "solutions" to these problems that are congruent with the capitalist organization of society. The people benefitting from the Ontario Works program are not social assistance recipients; rather the beneficiaries are the social relations of capital, state relations and employers.

Neoliberalism and moral regulation are also linked between capitalism and state relations because, in the case of the Ontario Works program, state relations devised this program consistent with the neoliberal agenda in that it pushes people to work for low wages. This provides an advantage to employers as they compete on a global scale. The program also serves to morally regulate people living in poverty by enforcing work norms and producing "good," disciplined workers.

Figure 6.1 Map of Social Relations

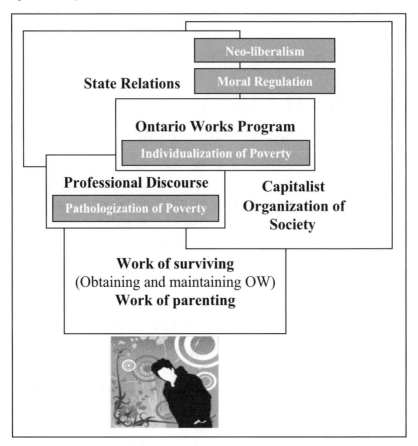

Near the top of the map we see the Ontario Works program, which is far reaching and includes a number of organizations beyond state relations. It encompasses the people working at the level of the Ministry of Community and Social Services, the delivery agents, the brokers and the participating organizations (although the extent to which they participate in the discourse varies). It also includes key documents, such as Ontario Works legislation and Policy Directives and the service contracts and funding arrangements that involve municipalities and non-government organizations with the program.

The Ontario Works program is connected to state relations because they are responsible for translating ruling ideologies into social policies and programs like Ontario Works. As evidenced by earlier discussions, these ruling ideologies used by state relations are influenced by the capitalist organization of society. The Ontario Works program is also tied to the capitalist organization of society because it provides subsidized labour to employers and enforces work norms to produce disciplined workers.

The Ontario Works program itself connects to professional discourse because it affects how the "problem" of poverty is professionalized and bureaucratized and it affects the resulting professional discourse. The individualization of poverty is an important feature of the Ontario Works program that impacts how the social problem of poverty is addressed, i.e., it shifts blame for poverty towards the individual and obscures the social and structural relations that produce poverty. The resulting professional discourse thus focuses interventions on the individual and does not address larger social relations.

State or ruling ideologies are enacted through professional discourse, which shapes social assistance services. Professional discourse shapes how staff working in the area of social assistance view recipients and how they are taught to "help" them. The institutional ideologies are learned and used to make sense of people's experience. Under professional discourse we see the pathologization of poverty, because with the way social assistance programs such as Ontario Works operate, poverty is seen as a sort of disease, which can be treated by professionals. The pathologization of poverty is also related to the individualization of poverty as it looks for fault with the individual. In the case of Ontario Works, poverty is seen as being caused by issues such as lack of motivation and poor hygiene (which is largely tied to moral regulation), and thus attempts at "treating" poverty become concerned with these individual issues as opposed to the larger social relations that force people into poverty.

The bottom box in Figure 6.1 represents the work that social assistance recipients must do, both as it relates to their own survival and to the survival of their children through their work as parents. This work is shaped by professional discourse and the Ontario Works program. The work of survival in this case largely encompasses the tasks that accompany the receipt of social assistance: for instance, the work of proving oneself worthy of assistance — both initially and on an ongoing basis, and the work of complying with the requirements imposed by case workers and brokers, such as job searches and community and employment placements. This work is tied to how the program attempts to morally regulate social assistance recipients and enforce work norms. The work of parenting is also influenced by a person receiving social assistance. The parents I spoke to told me about watching their children be disappointed because they could not afford what others had; the children of social assistance recipients were socially excluded from participating in community and school activities because of their parents' financial situation; and these children and youth struggle to escape the social relations that push their parents into poverty.

At the bottom of the diagram is a person. This person represents the social assistance recipients, who on a daily basis must face and confront the Ontario Works program. The shapes and images behind the person are meant to represent the other factors that affect the person's life (such as gender, ethnicity, race, language, (dis)ability and illness), which in turn affect their work of surviving and parenting. Looking at the social map as a whole highlights the extent to which each and every level plays a part in determining the class location of social assistance recipients. As Ng (1998) and Thompson (1966) argue, class is not a simple category; rather, it is a dynamic process and is largely determined by where people are located in their lives and the struggles they are involved in. The location of social assistance recipients and the struggles they get involved in on a daily basis are largely shaped by their relationship to the Ontario Works program and the work of the social relations at play in organizing this program.

Using the notion of social relations to investigate and map the Ontario Works program shows how problems are experienced and ultimately tied to the capitalist organization of society. This notion of social relations is useful because it allows us to see how the problems that social assistance recipients experience are not necessarily because, for example, a person has a "bad" case worker. The problems go much deeper and therefore the work that needs to be done to change the system needs to go much further than the Ontario Works program. The roots of the problem lie with the capitalist organization of society.

CONTRIBUTIONS AND IMPLICATIONS OF THIS STUDY

From the experiential accounts of social assistance recipients it is clear that major problems exist with the Ontario Works program and how it operates. This is evidenced by the disjuncture between how some social assistance recipients experience the program as a modern-day form of slavery and how the institutional standpoint purports that this program is intended to "help" social assistance recipients. This disjuncture is connected to how the Ontario Works program is socially organized. Despite claiming to "help meet the needs" of people on social assistance, the research participants demonstrated that it actually exploits people living in poverty on Ontario Works for the benefit of employers and the social relations of capital.

Starting from the standpoint of social assistance recipients, we see some of the problems that emerge in their everyday lives and how these are tied to the larger social relations that push them into poverty, and leave them relying on Ontario Works to survive. These include issues such as the lack of social support for and recognition for the work parents/women do in raising children, lack of available employment, lack of jobs with living wages and health benefits, limited access to opportunities for higher education (for recipients and their children) and discrimination from employers based on age and appearance. These barriers are social in nature and are not recognized or addressed within the framework of the Ontario Works program. This is because the institutional ideology of Ontario Works (consistent with neoliberal discourse) views the barriers to employment as being related to the individual and therefore completely ignores the social relations that produce poverty.

Because of the institutional failure to see the social roots of poverty, the focus on getting people off welfare translates into getting jobs, developing motivation and other individual features. When getting jobs becomes the only priority and jobs end up as the objectives and outcomes of welfare programs, the social relations at play in determining people's social locations become obscured, and other important dimensions like ensuring a living wage, finding safe, affordable housing and ensuring health benefits get lost.

The way the Ontario Works program is formulated, it comes to be a program for meeting the needs of the social relations of capital by enforcing work norms through administrative obstacles, by providing a "lesson" to those who work for wages that their fate on assistance would be worse, by stigmatizing social assistance recipients and by exerting pressure on recipients to work for low wages. The program further meets the needs of the social relations of capital through the practices that make up the program; these limit access to educational opportunities, which some recipients felt would help them to secure decent employment, and also make it difficult to actually provide opportunities for valuable training to social assistance recipients. The combination of these factors highlights the extent to which the Ontario Works program, state agencies and a number of other actors involved with the administration of the program come to meet the needs of the social relations of capital, at the expense of social assistance recipients.

The research participants have shown me that the way the Ontario Works program is socially organized is not about helping to meet the needs of social assistance recipients, but rather it is about enforcing work norms to ensure people are forced to work for low wages, all the while expanding moral regulation through the help of organizations normally outside the reach of state relations. Furthermore, this program provides subsidies to a number of employers for hiring social assistance recipients, it provides free labour to employers through the different placement programs, and it pressures social assistance recipients to accept low-wage work, in addition to serving as a means of morally regulating the lives of people on social assistance.

The fact that the Ontario Works program does nothing to address the class location of social assistance recipients is tied to the nature of state reforms that deal with issues of class struggle. Teeple (1995) argues that social reforms emerge as a means of alleviating some of the results of class struggle, but that they are fundamentally flawed because they manage and regulate class struggle from the standpoint of capital. This is in part because, as Smith (1987) argues, the issue of class conflict, which is at the core of these struggles, is removed from the picture through the process of bureaucratization and professionalization. Addressing poverty through these processes results in poverty becoming separated from the realities of class relations and capitalism. Through these processes the root causes are obscured, and it becomes impossible to address the situation because proposed solutions avoid the roots of the problem.

The failure of reforms to address the root causes of poverty is evidenced by the persistence of poverty despite social programs and reforms that have been made by different governments over the years. The poverty rate[1] in Ontario of 14 percent in 1980 remains the same in 2003. Although there has been some variation in the poverty rate during this period,[2] the number has never reached a single digit, which means that there are always at least 10 percent of the people in Ontario living in poverty (National Council of Welfare 2006: 31). At the national level, despite a unanimous vote in 1989 by members of the House of Commons to end child poverty by 2000, the rate in 2003 (18 percent) is higher than the rate in 1989 (15 percent) when the vote was passed (National Council of Welfare 2006: 3). Until social reforms and programs address the root causes of poverty it will continue to exist.

The participants in this study have shown me that through programs such as Ontario Works, people on social assistance have priorities imposed upon them that do not necessarily correspond with their own priorities, and as a result they experience a number of problems in their lives. The priorities imposed upon them focus largely on forcing attachments to the waged labour force, under the guise of attempting to secure employment and "getting off" welfare. My analysis reveals the actual purpose of workfare programs, which has nothing to do with providing people sustainable jobs. Instead it is a general attack on people on social assistance, while providing subsidized and cheap labour for some companies and social agencies. The precarious and transient forms of labour are not going to produce any major benefits in these peoples' lives.

From the institutional perspective of Ontario Works, success is simply measured by the number of placements or "jobs" and decreasing caseloads. The actual circumstances in which people find themselves once they leave Ontario Works are overlooked. This is evidenced by the fact that there has been no government-funded follow-up to track or evaluate the outcomes of people leaving the Ontario Works program (Workfare Watch 2002). In order to understand the situations in which people are finding themselves once they leave assistance we must rely on other sources, such as the follow-up telephone survey of social assistance leavers (n=804) commissioned by the City of Toronto in 2001. This study reports:

> Approximately 56 percent of the respondents to the Toronto survey reported that they left assistance for either their own or a spouse's "employment related reasons" (which included beginning a new job or returning to a previous job, obtaining a better job, or getting a raise, promotion or more hours at work). A further 11 percent left for what may be loosely termed "system reasons": ineligibility, didn't want to stay on assistance,

or had difficulty with the bureaucracy. The remainder reported leaving for other reasons including receiving another government benefit (8 per cent), family or households reasons (6 per cent) or starting school (6 per cent). (Lightman, Mitchell and Herd 2005: 98)[3]

Of those who left for employment reasons, at the time of the survey 16 percent had changed jobs and 14 percent had lost their job and were unemployed. Of those who were employed at the time of the survey, 37 percent were earning less that $10 an hour (considered below the threshold of poverty). The authors also report that the jobs obtained by social assistance leavers are of a poor nature, providing little stability or benefits; 30 percent were temporary and 28 percent were part-time. The fact that many people find themselves in precarious work situations signifies that they will most likely end up returning to social assistance once their jobs are finished.

SOCIAL ASSISTANCE AND WORKFARE PROGRAMS

This shift in requiring social assistance recipients to labour for their benefits also completely overshadows the other work that they do within their lives. The research participants all did parenting work, and a number of them had part-time jobs or were already volunteering with local organizations to serve their communities. Similarly, 45 percent of social assistance recipients are parents,[4] and 12 percent of Ontario Works recipients are also working for wages.[5] This work that social assistance recipients do (in particular the unwaged work) is completely ignored.

Social assistance policy should be changed to recognize the work that recipients are already doing and the contributions that this work (including non-waged work) brings to their community. People need to be acknowledged for the work they do and they need to be supported to ensure they are able to continue with it. The neoliberal ideologies on which workfare programs are based are disconnected from the everyday lived realities of people on social assistance. It is only by grounding training and employment programs in the actual, everyday lived realities of people that programs can be responsive to the needs of these people. The institutional ideologies that underlie social assistance programs cannot be detached from the realities of peoples' lives. This failure inevitably produces problems for people on social assistance.

SOCIAL ASSISTANCE RECIPIENTS

Under the "ruling relations" of neoliberalism, the barriers to employment that people are seen as facing are considered to be individual barriers, for example, lack of motivation. The truth is that these barriers are far larger and are social in character. To change these requires work at the social level, not primarily at the individual level. If the intent of workfare programs were genuinely to get people into jobs so that they are able to stay off assistance then it would be wise to ask individual recipients about the actual barriers they face to employment. The participants I spoke with had no trouble articulating the things that prevented them from securing employment. Social assistance recipients are in the best possible position to articulate these barriers and their actual needs because they know these through their lived experiences.

My analyses have highlighted the fact that there needs to be change in how people living in poverty on Ontario Works are socially constructed through state and media discourse. They need to be portrayed in a way that more accurately reflects their everyday lives; they are not lazy and undeserving. These are people struggling to get by with limited resources, and they face a number of systemic and social barriers. Meanwhile, the work they do and their genuine attempts to contribute to their community through volunteer work, part-time work or parenting work are not recognized by current welfare programs.

FURTHER RESEARCH IS NECESSARY

This investigation is only a preliminary institutional ethnographic analysis, which in some ways only scratches the surface of the relations explored here. The amount of research and analysis that was possible within the confines of a master's thesis is limited. Given the amount of data collected for this project, and the richness of the data itself, there is much more that can be investigated regarding how the Ontario Works program is socially organized and how this creates problems in the lives of recipients. One of the obvious issues that was beyond the scope of this book but that merits being addressed is the extent to which the experiences of people on social assistance are mediated by gender, ethnicity, race, language, (dis)ability and illness.

Some of the other issues that emerged and merit more attention are the mothering and parenting work that social assistance recipients do and the impacts on children and young people. Further attention should be paid to how the problems social assistance recipients face penetrate into the lives of their children. More attention should also be paid to how women get forced into poverty because of relationship breakdowns. Also there could be more investigation of the struggles that organizations faced in deciding whether or not to accept social assistance recipients on placement.

RECOMMENDATIONS FOR CHANGE

Based on the experiences of the research participants there are a number of ways in which the Ontario Works program (or other social assistance programs) could be changed to make it better for recipients. Many flow out of what I learned from Ontario Works recipients themselves. I briefly outline some of the recommendations for change here. These recommendations are only a beginning of what is needed in getting at the social roots of poverty, which are tied to the relations of a capitalist society.

1. Social assistance rates need to be increased to ensure that recipients can afford safe housing, along with other necessities such as food, transportation and decent clothing. Rates should be sufficient to ensure that people on social assistance are provided with enough to participate in necessary social and educational activities.

   > Jane: You don't get enough money. I mean it wasn't so bad before Mike Harris took over and changed it all and reduced our "allowance" as they call it. But now it's really bad. Before it was a day before we ran out of money and food and we could handle one day before cheques came in. Now it's like four or five days, sometimes a week, depending on how the month goes.

2. Supports need to be put in place to ensure that the children of Ontario Works recipients are not pushed further into relations of poverty. This includes assisting them in accessing higher education and removing punitive regulations that force these young people to move out if they leave school. Also, if a youth wants to live at home

while going to college or university, they should be allowed to do so without having to pay half the rent.

3. The work that social assistance recipients are already doing and the contributions they are already making to their communities, including reproductive and domestic labour, need to be acknowledged. In particular, the parenting work that they do and the contributions this makes to their children need to be valued, especially given the lack of affordable child care. Correspondingly, the amount of work required for social assistance recipients needs to be minimized, for instance, eliminating the work requirement, reducing the number of documents recipients must obtain during the application process, reducing travel barriers by having brokers located at the delivery agency, and eliminating unnecessary steps in the placement application process, such as criminal reference checks.

4. Welfare programs should be changed to assist and support recipients to access higher education, if they feel this would help to meet their needs. Jane outlines some of the problems Ontario Works produces in this area.

> Work for welfare was made to get people that are on welfare to get out there and get some experience. And hopefully the employer will end up hiring you in the end... So you got this experience now, no papers [certificate/degree] to back you up and if you want your education, well you screwed up the first time so you're pretty much screwed unless you want to take out a huge loan, and who's going to give you a loan when you've got nothing for collateral?

5. The privacy, respect and dignity of social assistance recipients need to be maintained by eliminating the social practices currently in place. These include requiring a criminal check to obtain placements and treating recipients differently than "regular" employees.

6. Workfare programs such as Ontario Works should not exist because they are mandatory and coercive. Rather these should be replaced with voluntary employment and training programs. Clearly the type of "assistance" provided through employment and training programs do not meet the needs of all social assistance recipients.

Therefore, employment and training programs should be voluntary and should only be used where a recipient indicates it might be helpful in addressing some of their needs.

> Margaret: Like I said, I don't think it's [social assistance] one size fits all. The government has expectations that everybody who goes to this work for your welfare cheque is actually going to do it for a while and then get off it because you got a job. And that's not the case and there's a big gap between those who can go out and get a job, and those who don't have skills like literacy, self esteem, are not mature enough to go out and get a job, don't have personal development skills to get a job.

7. Safeguards need to be implemented to ensure that placements provided through employment programs are valuable for social assistance recipients and that they meet their needs, as opposed to those of employers.

> Danielle: The theory [behind Ontario Works] is that you would get some kind of training for a possible job and improve your work skills. That I always found questionable because the big one [placement experience] that they kept promoting was tree planting. I mean I'm sorry, but how many jobs are going to be available in tree planting?

8. Employment and training programs need to encourage investment in skill development and provide opportunities for meaningful experiences. Recipients have told me that despite their willingness to continue on with placements, the rules of the program surrounding length of placements often make it impossible. Employers also reported that it is not in their best interests to invest in training recipients on placement to learn new skills because placements are for such limited periods of time that there is no return on the investment. The timeline for employment programs should be extended to ensure they are of sufficient duration to provide a return on the training investment of the employer, while providing valuable experience for the recipient.

9. Ontario Works should not take 50 percent of wages from part-time work off a recipient's welfare benefits. The formula should ensure that there is an encouragement for people to work for wages.

Jack: That half of the wages [from part-time employment being deducted from our monthly assistance], it shouldn't be there at all.

Melissa: 'Cause people are trying. I know they [the government] are trying to encourage people into doing what's best and finding work, but chopping the whole half [of the wages], that's the only disagreement I have, that won't encourage them at all.

The Ontario Works program is organized to meet the needs of the social relations of capital and of employers at the expense of people living in poverty. There are a number of ways that have been outlined above that can change the Ontario Works program for the better, but these are only minor fixes as they do not address the root causes of poverty. To address the issue of poverty we need to challenge and change the capitalist organization of society.

NOTES

1. Defined by the number of people living below the Low-Income Cut-Offs (LICO), an unofficial measure of poverty in Canada.
2. The poverty rate for Ontario between 1980 and 2003 ranged from a low of 11 percent in 1989 to a high of 19 percent in 1996, with the average poverty rate for this time period being 15 percent (National Council of Welfare 2006: 31).
3. One of the biggest flaws with this survey was the low response rate; out of a potential 3,335 respondents only 804 interviews were conducted (24 percent). This is partly attributable to the living conditions that many social assistance recipients face as a result of the Ontario Works program. We know, at least anecdotally, that many people have been evicted because they have not been able to pay the rent; some people have ended up on the streets; others have gone to live with family, and some women have returned to violent partners because of the cuts to welfare benefits (see Little 2003). Also, since the survey was conducted over the telephone, those without a telephone were excluded. These flaws do not necessarily undermine the validity of the results; rather they probably speak to the extent to which the percentage that got employment is inflated.
4. In March 2005, 36 percent of Ontario Works cases were single parents, while 9 percent of cases were couples with dependent children. This represents close to half (45 percent) of all Ontario Works cases that are involved in the socially necessary work of raising children (Human Resources and Social Development Canada, 2006).

5. In March 2008 approximately 12 percent of Ontario Works cases across the province (24,024 cases) were declaring earnings from working for wages. It is however unknown how many of these people were also required to participate in employment assistance activities in addition to this paid work (personal email communication with an Ontario Works administrator).

REFERENCES

Blake, Raymond B., and Jeffrey A. Keshen (eds.). 2006. *Social Fabric or Patchwork Quilt: The Development of Social Policy in Canada*. Peterborough, ON: Broadview Press.

Citizens on the Web–News. 1999. "Quixote's Horse: Workfare — A Little History." Available at <home.cogeco.ca/~wcoppin/workfare.html> accessed on 24/06/2008.

Gervais, Lisa. 1996. "Poverty Group Quits Workfare Committee." *Sudbury Star*, August 27.

Goffman, Erving. 1963. *Stigma: Notes on the Management of Spoiled Identity*. New York: J. Aronson.

Guest, Dennis. 1997. *The Emergence of Social Security in Canada* (Third edition). Vancouver: UBC Press.

Harris, Mike. 1995. "The Common Sense Revolution." Toronto.

Human Resources and Social Development Canada. 2006. "Social Assistance Statistical Report 2005: Chapter 8 — Ontario Works." Available at <hrsdc. gc.ca/en/cs/sp/sdc/socpol/publications/reports/sd10-3-2004e/page10. shtml> accessed on 08/08/2008.

Kinsman, Gary. 2005. "The Politics of Revolution: Learning from Autonomist Marxism." *Upping the Ante: A Journal of Theory and Action*. Available at <uppingtheanti.org/node/383> accessed on 24/06/2008.

Lightman, Ernie, Andrew Mitchell, and Dean Herd. 2005. "Welfare to What? After Workfare in Toronto." *International Social Security Review* 58, 4.

Little, Margaret. 1998. *'No Car, No Radio, No Liquor Permit': The Moral Regulation of Single Mothers in Ontario, 1920–1997*. Toronto: Oxford University Press.

_____. 2003. "The Leaner, Meaner Welfare Machine: The Ontario Conservative Government's Ideological and Material Attack on Single Mothers." In Deborah Brock (ed.), *Making Normal: Social Regulation in Canada*. Toronto: Nelson Thomson Learning.

Ministry of Community and Social Services. 2004. "Auditor's Report, Section 3.03: Ontario Disability Support Program." Available at <auditor.on.ca/en/reports_en/en04/303en04.pdf> accessed on 08/08/2008.

_____. 2007. "About Ontario Works." Available at <mcss.gov.on.ca/mcss/english/pillars/social/programs/ow.htm> accessed on 02/12/2007.

_____. 2008. "Ontario Works Employment Assistance Quarterly Report December 2007." Internal Planning document.

Mykhalovskiy, Eric, and George Smith. 1994. *Hooking Up to Social Services: A Report on the Barriers People Living with HIV/AIDS Face Accessing Social Services*. Toronto: Ontario Institute for Studies in Education.

National Council of Welfare. 2006. "Poverty Profile, 2002 and 2003." Available at <ncwcnbes.net/documents/researchpublications/ResearchProjects/PovertyProfile/2002-03Report_Summer2006/ReportENG.pdf> accessed on 08/08/2008.

Ng, Roxanna. 1998. *The Politics of Community Services: Immigrant Woman, Class and State* (Second edition). Halifax: Fernwood Publishing.

Ontario Works Policy Directives. 2008. Available at <accesson.ca/mcss/english/pillars/social/ow-directives/ow_policy_directives.htm> accessed on 31/03/2008.

Piven, Frances Fox, and Richard Cloward. 1993. *Regulating the Poor: The Functions of Public Welfare*. New York: Vintage Books.

Quaid, Maeve. 2002. *Workfare: Why Good Social Policy Ideas Go Bad*. Toronto: University of Toronto Press.

Renaud, Marc. 1975. "On the Structural Constraints to State Interventions Health." *International Journal of Health Services* 5, 4: 559–71.

Smith, Dorothy. 1987. *The Everyday World as Problematic: A Feminist Sociology*. Toronto: University of Toronto Press.

_____ (ed.). 2006. *Institutional Ethnography as Practice*. Lanham, MD: Rowan and Littlefield Publishers.

Smith, Dorothy, and George Smith. 1990. "Re-organizing the Job-skills Training Relation: From 'Human Capital' to 'Human Resources.'" In Jacob Muller (ed.), *Canada's Changing Community Colleges*. Toronto: Garamond Press.

St. Pierre, Denis. 1996a. "Activists Rip into Workfare." *Sudbury Star*, September 10.

_____. 1996b. "Local Politicians Won't Oppose Workfare." *Sudbury Star*, September 10.

Sudbury Coalition for Social Justice. 1999. "Statement in Response to the Announcement by Janet Ecker Concerning the Introduction of Workfare into the Private Sector." Sudbury: Sudbury Coalition for Social Justice.

Teeple, Gary. 1995. *Globalization and the Decline of Social Reform*. Toronto: Garamond Press.

Thompson, Edward P. 1966. *The Making of the English Working Class*. New York: Vintage Books.

Whitehouse, Mike. 1996a. "Poverty Group's Representative Resigns from Workfare Committee." *Northern Life* August 27.

_____. 1996b. "Little Resolved at Public Forum on Workfare." *Northern Life* September, 11.

_____. 1996c. "Workfare Start Date Delayed a Year." *Northern Life* September, 30.

Workfare Watch. 2002. "Tracking the Outcomes of Welfare Reform: Bulletin #15." Toronto: Ontario Social Safety Network and the Community Social Planning Council of Toronto.